Dedication

My entire life, I always wanted to write. Poetry, children's stories or short stories but a novel was my ultimate goal. Many people have supported me, encouraged me, and made me believe in my abilities. These people include everyone from teachers, friends, family and even those I've never met on social media. It would be impossible to dedicate this book to only one or even a few of those people. Therefore, I dedicate this book to everyone that crossed my path leaving a positive footprint. Words can't express my gratitude for having you all in my life.

Prologue

The characters and events in this book are based on real people and my personal true story. However, the names of people and places have been changed. The events depicted have been edited to enhance the storyline. Not every event or situation is completely factual. Some things have been omitted, others an addition.

I have wanted to write my story for many years, but I also wanted to protect the people that may have been victimised.

It is true, everyone has their own demons or secrets in their closet, some we choose to let go of and others we take to our graves. Millie's journey depicts, to the best of my ability, my life and the edited secrets I was willing to release.

There are chapters that will include sexual, emotional and physical abuse, as well as curse words. I therefore recommend a reading age of no less than 16 years.

Thank you for taking this journey with me and I wish you a life of happiness and peace! Always!

Table of Contents

Chapter One

Childhood isn't always easy

I don't want to... Millie wasn't sure if she had said the words out load, but it didn't matter anyway, Mr. Ward wasn't giving her an opportunity to choose whether or not this was what she wanted. His hands were huge, they completely covered Millie's upper leg as he adjusted her on his lap. The smell of cigarette butts, beer and motor oil filled her nostrils as she took deep, slow breaths to try and stop herself from crying.

Mr. Ward was inside looking at a magazine as Millie and Danny opened the creaky wooden door.

"Hi guys," Mr. Ward smiled at the two inquisitive children. "You want to see the race car? Go ahead Danny, you can get inside." The greasy smelly old man lifted Danny up through the roll cage and onto the bucket seat inside. He then returned to his chair and instructed Millie to come over to him.

At 8 years old Millie didn't object, she was always taught to do what she was told, but when Mr. Ward lifted her onto his lap, she knew something just didn't feel right. Her tummy flipped around, and her body tensed up. Holding a small child in place on your lap was effortless when your hand covered her entire thigh. He placed his other hand firmly around Millie's waist, then he shifted himself until he was satisfied with her position.

"Ever seen these types of magazines?" Mr. Wards' dirty hand lifted from her thigh long enough to move the magazine along the dirty counter closer to her view.

What Millie saw, when she took a quick glance frightened her, even though she didn't really understand what it was she was looking at. She wanted to cry, she wanted to scream, she wanted to shout for him to let her down. Instead, she just shook her head side to side. "That's a shame," he continued, "you might learn something."

The magazine Mr. Ward was showing her contained images of ladies wearing no clothes, they were smiling but Millie didn't understand how those girls could be happy. After all someone was taking pictures of them completely naked.

She looked over to see if her brother had finally finished playing but he was nowhere to be seen. His 12-year-old body was completely hidden inside the stupid black car.

Mr. Ward continued moving Millie around on his lap, she felt something rising under her bottom and it was at that moment she struggled to get down. His grip tightened around her waist, and she felt him breathing heavier, his hot breath flowing down the nape of her neck.

"Don't go anywhere, don't you like sitting with me" he paused for just a moment. If he was waiting for a reply, he wasn't getting one. "You know Millie, little girls should wear dresses," he grunted as he moved his hand along Millie's thigh, his thumb touching between her legs. Never had Millie been so thankful she was wearing jeans. Even then it was the most disgusting dirty thing she had ever experienced.

With the other hand still around her waist he crawled his fingers up her shirt touching her undeveloped breast.

Just as Millie was no longer able to hold back her tears, her brothers head appeared from the window area of the car.

"That was so cool!" Danny shouted, struggling to get out. Mr. Ward lifted Millie off his lap and went to help her brother. "Come on Mills, let's go collect rocks." Danny bounded toward the door.

Wiping away the only tear that managed to escape her eyes, Millie sniffed, and held back her emotions.

The two youngsters ran off into the fields behind the garage. Millie never told anyone about what Mr. Ward did to her then or any other time he was able to get her in the garage. At least it never came out while she was a child anyway. Millie was humiliated and felt disgusting. She had never hated anyone so much in her short life. Eventually that and a whole lot more would surface, but for now it was Millie's little (big) secret.

The town Millie grew up in was her absolute favourite place in the world, not that she had been many places. Her family did move home quite often but that never really bothered her. She always made new friends easily and found it fun to get a new bedroom and find new areas outside to explore. Her town of Welling would always be home, no matter what happened or where life took her.

Millie grew up in a home life that many would call unstable, her parents fought all the time and she choose to explore outside as her way of getting away from it all. Down the road and along a path from that house with the red garage, Mills found a grassy open area near a river, and it immediately became her new secret spot. A place where she could go to be all alone.

"Can I have a bowl of sugar?" Millie asked her mother smiling. Her sweet little freckled face was hard for her mom to resist. Knowing exactly what she wanted it for, her mother grabbed a bowl from the cupboard and poured in a few tablespoons of white sugar.

"Don't forget to bring back my bowl!" Her mom always complained that the bowls kept going missing, Millie, guilty, probably had three of them by the river already.

Mills ran out the door with her bowl and walked down the road toward her secret spot. The neighbour had lots of rhubarb plants and told Millie and Danny; they could help themselves whenever they wanted. It was pure heaven, sitting by the river, dipping her rhubarb into the sugar, seemingly without a care in the world. She took off her shoes, sat down on a rock and let her feet dangle in the water, it was cold but refreshing.

The summer holidays went by quickly and Millie was so excited that September had finally rolled around again. School was an important part of Millie's life, she loved to learn and did very well in all her classes. She had a lot of friends, but one in particular, was very special.

Paula was Millies best friend, they had met in kindergarten at just 4 years of age, when Paula helped a shy Millie emerge from her hiding spot in the corner. They knew then, they would be friends forever. Not only did they spend all day together at school but every weekend one could be found at the others home, having sleepovers or doing anything and everything their little hearts desired. Paula, just like Millie had to always make sure the house was clean before being allowed out, so as soon as one was finished her household duties, she would then go to the others home to help. The girls soon became part of each other's families and considered themselves not only best friends, but sisters from different parents.

Paula was the only one to know Millie's secrets, the ones that she cared to share anyway and with her best friend by her side Millie always felt safe.

Or maybe somewhat safe.

Across from Millies house was a school, a catholic school for that matter, where if you went inside and looked at the staff photos you would find a picture of the one and only Mr. Ward, teacher of grade 8 English. Yes Mr. Paedophile was a schoolteacher, at a Catholic school no less.

Outside, there was a small playground where the girls spent a lot of their time after school or on weekends.

Paula's dad was a bit of an asshole, he insisted on Paula pretty much doing everything. Millie went over to help her one Saturday. Afterk finishing the chores the girls went to hang out at the school playground before going back to Millie's for dinner.

"Who the heck is that?" Paula motioned toward the parking lot where a white pickup truck had entered. Mills just shrugged but found it quite odd that a middle-aged man was going to a school playground, alone. Trying not to be too obvious the girls watched him as he walked toward the playground and approached them. He wore grey track suit bottoms and an oversized T shirt; he smiled at the young girls.

"Hello, nice day, eh?" The man nodded leaning against the monkey bars. He must've been in his 30's, and he gave the girls bad vibes immediately. "Yea," both girls chimed together and shared a giggle at the man's expense, turning away from him.

He rose his hands above his head and grabbed onto the bars above him. Letting out a light cough he grabbed the girl's attention.
"Mills, let's go!" Paula grabbed Millie by the hand and demanded to leave. Looking over at the man to see what all the fuss was about, Millie soon understood. As the man raised his arms his T-shirt lifted up and visible to the girls was a large hole cut out in the man's tracksuit bottoms, exposing his penis to them. At 9 years old neither girl had even seen a penis, except that of maybe Paula's little brothers or Millie's baby nephew, but not like this.

Without saying another word, the girls started to walk off heading in the direction of Millie's house, which was just over the hill at the edge of the school yard.

The man stood and watched the girls for only a moment or two, then proceeded to head back toward his truck. "He's going to come after us," Paula was obviously scared, her eyes widened and started to water. Millie held her hand and encouraged her saying that they were not far from home and just to keep going. As the girls reached the top of the hill and were about to cross the road, they noticed the white truck. Their little legs never moved so fast as they ran across the front yard and into the house. Millie pulled the curtain open, just a little and they watched. The man turned his truck around in the road that led to the red garage, then he drove off. The girls went upstairs to Millie's room and collapsed on the bed. The weird thing is, it was never spoken of again. In fact, through the years Millie often wondered if it was all a dream. She never asked Paula if it really happened, but she also had never had a dream that she was able to recall so vividly.

Luckily, the next few years would be fairly uneventful, Millie spent her time hanging out with her friends, focusing on her schoolwork and avoiding Mr. Ward at all costs. Her sister Sarah had a son and at 3 years old he had become like a little brother to Millie. She loved playing with him and helping to take care of him too. He wasn't there all the time as her sister spent half the time at her boyfriend's house, her nephew, being raised between the two parents' homes.

Danny was getting older too and started hanging out with boys that caused a lot of trouble, it wasn't long before he was in trouble himself and the police knocked on the door. After a stern warning, the police officers left, and a huge fight started between her parents. Millie ran into the living room and sat tucked in a ball at the corner of the sofa.

Millie's dad was an angry man and sometimes even the smallest of things would set him off. Millie's mom on the other hand, defended her son with a simple, boys will be boys. "I'm sick of you protecting the little fucker," her dad screamed, "he's becoming a proper little shit, next thing you know he's going to be in jail, then what?" Her mom didn't answer, instead she rolled her eyes and started to walk away.

Millie's dad opened the cupboard and suddenly a plate flew across the room, Mills closed her eyes tight. The yelling was deafening and even at 12 years old now Millie was very afraid. She knew how this would end, and it wouldn't be the first time either. Millie's mom on a few different occasions had told the children to pack their belongings, she was taking them and leaving. Mills didn't blame her but she was still terrified every time it happened because she knew they had nowhere to go.

When Millie was 9, they had moved to a different town just for one year, but during that year she had to change schools. It was ok as she met a new friend but that was the home where her parents had a huge fight. Sarah, Danny and Millie were instructed by their mom to pack their clothes in garbage bags. She was leaving their dad. Millie dragged her garbage bag down the stairs while trying to hold her doll. With 3 children and 3 bags by the front door, Millie's dad blocked the way so they couldn't leave. Millie was crying, she had no idea where they would go. She envisioned them being homeless, maybe they could get a tent and live by her river.
It wasn't to happen as eventually they were told to take the bags back upstairs. Disaster averted; they wouldn't be homeless quite yet.

Eventually the fighting stopped, and Millie's mom was left on the kitchen floor crying, clutching at her throat. Had her dad tried to strangle her mom? He grabbed his keys, walked out the door, got into the car and drove off. Danny, who was hiding in his room, came running downstairs as soon as he heard the car leave. "I hate him," Danny yelled at the front door. The children helped their mom up off the floor and into the living room where she could sit down. Danny was subject to their fathers' anger more than either of the girls. He was a bit of a smart mouth and their dad taught discipline by using his belt more than a few times. Millie would hide in her room listening to him yelling at Danny, hearing the snap of the belt on Danny's backside while he cried.

(Every once in a while, I may interrupt your reading with something that is on my mind, right now I'd like to focus on abuse, sexual, physical and emotional. The statistics you see or hear in the media, for example, rape, sexual assault or sexual abuse happens to 1 in 4 women, 1 in 6 children and 1 in 18 men, are reported cases. As you are seeing in my story not everyone tells someone. So, these figures are scary when you think how many go unreported. I don't have a reason why I didn't report anything that happened to me, I can't tell you why. In some cases, I believe that when this happens as a child, and it happens more than once by different people it becomes an almost 'normal' part of life. As horrific as this is, it's a reality we need to be aware of. So, when 1 in 6 children are affected by this type of abuse, I know in my heart these figures as actually a lot higher. Please take care of your loved ones and instil in your children the importance of 'good touch vs bad touch'. Every child has the right to a safe and happy childhood.)

Danny went to the kitchen to make their mom a cup of coffee and Millie picked up the phone and called her sister. After telling Sarah what had happened, she hung up and knew Sarah would be on her way over to help look after their mom. Once Sarah arrived, they were all able to talk and find out exactly what had happened.
The police had caught a now 16-year-old Danny and his friends breaking into the school across the street. They weren't going to pursue anything because they had been caught before any real damage was done, but they still came to make sure he was disciplined by his parents. Millie's dad was always very hard on Danny, but her mother had eyes that could only see the angel in her son. You couldn't blame her really, she was in protection mode most of the time.

The plan was set in motion again for them to leave, this time it was seriously going to happen. Her mom was going to call family benefits and get help. Although she used to work full time, for the past few years she hadn't worked at all. She would need help to afford a place for them to live. Then, when it was all set up, they would move out while her dad was at work.

Millie started to cry, not knowing what the best decision was, but imagining her father coming home to an empty house pulled at her heart strings. She hated the way her dad got angry all the time, she wanted the fighting, the yelling, the name calling to end but she loved her dad and could only think of his sadness on the day he would be all alone.

Two months later, everything was arranged, Danny and Millie stayed off school to help. Her dad had left for work at 7am and at 7:30 the moving van was in the driveway. The house was left with just enough furniture for her father including one plate, one fork and one spoon. Danny and their mother climbed into the moving truck while Millie ran upstairs to grab one last thing. Her doll that her dad had bought her for her 4th birthday. She stopped for a moment holding her doll, the sadness in her heart was heavy and she started to cry. "I'm sorry daddy," she sobbed as she walked back down the stairs and climbed into the van beside her brother. Millie always had a sense of guilt for everything that happened in her life. She felt guilty she couldn't stop her father, guilty she couldn't protect her brother or her mom from his anger. Being the baby of the family, there really wasn't anything Millie could have done, she knew that. She watched the house with the red garage fall out of view as they drove away, her little nose pressed against the window.

Chapter 2

Tough life as a teenager

Her father coming home to that empty house nearly broke Millie's heart. Yea, it was true her dad could be downright horrid, but he was still the man that used to put her up on his shoulders, or hide the Easter treats under the sofa. He was the one who took Millie to the hospital when she had tonsillitis. He was her dad and she missed him. Danny may feel differently, he and Sarah were Millie's half siblings. Her mother had been married before, so they had a different father. Millie had only met their dad twice in her life, he lived in a different province. So, that made it difficult for him to visit. The same situation had happened with Millie's dad as well. He too was married before and had a daughter four years older than Millie. Sometimes Mills wondered about the sister she didn't know, Sally. Her dad used to visit Sally when she was little but over time the visits stopped. Millie had no idea why.

"Mills," Danny called from the livingroom. Millie had been in her room unpacking boxes. She opened her door and peaked around the corner. "Let's go get pizza." Danny smiled. Well, that didn't need to be repeated. Millie grabbed her shoes and ran out the door after her brother.

Millie grew to enjoy the time she lived with her mom, at the beginning anyway. Danny had moved in with a friend shortly after they had left her dad. For the last year, it had been just Millie and her mom.

Contact with her dad had pretty much stopped and Millie, although she missed him, was preoccupied with friends, now, being a typical 14-year-old, friends became the most important thing in her life. Her mother had started dating and every now and then Mills would come home to a strange man sitting at the dining room table, sipping his coffee, smiling at Mills like he actually belonged there. Usually they were very unkempt, Millie wondered if they knew how to work a toothbrush.
Her room had become a kind of hideaway, she had

no desire to interact with the men her mom would bring home, the next one was worse than the last.

Millie arrived home from school one day and went to turn on the lights, they didn't work. The T.v? Nothing. The stove? Nope. Well, it was obvious her mother hadn't paid the gas or electricity bill. Things had been getting worse and her mother was spending less and less time at home. Feeling hungry Millie opened the frig to get something to eat. A margarine container nearly empty and an open pack of lunch meat with the ends all hard and out of date by 3 days. Mills grabbed a slice of bread and dolloped it with mayo and mustard. Dinner was served. The next day, a room temperature can of creamed corn was on the menu. I need to get a job, she thought to herself, this is ridiculous.

Mills found a job babysitting and she worked at the local bar, washing dishes and taking clean plates out to the dining area. She was exhausted with school and working but she had to earn a little money to help buy food.
Millies mom would return home every few days with a bag of groceries, courtesy of the food bank and joining her was her gentleman caller of the week. At times, Mills would be asked to go with her mom to the food bank. Millie hated it there. There was no

need for it really, her mom received benefits and surely, they gave her enough money for food. Since her mom wasn't paying the bills, where was the money going?

Gambling was becoming her mother's new passion, which explained her lack of ability to provide a suitable home life for Millie. Bingo was her mom's chosen gambling venue which meant Tuesday and Thursday she could pretty much guarantee her mom wouldn't be home.

There was one particular Thursday evening that Millie would never forget. Her mom had left at 6pm to get the best seat at that night's bingo and Mills was searching the cupboards for something to eat. With her stomach growling, she had to settle for stale corn flakes and powdered milk, luckily her mom had this week's food bank donation. At 6:45 she heard a knock at the door. Which nearly startled the corn flakes right out of her hands. She opened the door to find Mr. Man of the week requesting to see her mother.

The familiar smell of stale cigarettes and beer entered her nostrils. "Hi, where's your mother? Oh man, I need a piss," He pushed right past her and headed straight for the bathroom. He questioned where her mom had gone again and when she would be back. Millie being truthful, told him she was at bingo and should be home around 10:30pm. When he was done in the bathroom, he lit a cigarette and sat down at the table, "I'll wait then."

Wait? What was he talking about it was only 7pm. Millie nodded, her eyebrows raised in a 'whatever dude' expression, and she retreated to her bedroom.

Five minutes later Millie was startled by her bedroom door being swung open, hitting the wall nearby, startling the cornflakes right out of her hand a second time.

Before she could say anything, she was being told to shut up! She stood up and was pushed back down onto her bed. Millie was angrier than she was scared at this point and cursed the man out, "who the fuck do you think you are?" She questioned him.

"Big language for a little girl," he said tapping his belt buckle. "Now shut up, or I'll use this and trust me, it'll hurt!" He started to undo his belt and Millie wasn't sure if he was going to beat her with it or if something even worse was about to happen.
Her anger turned to fear, and Millie didn't know how to react. She remained quiet and curled herself up in the corner of the bed, hugging her knees into her

chest. He grabbed hold of her feet and pulled her down the bed, immediately covering her mouth with his disgusting hand, which he hadn't even washed after he had used the bathroom. He pinned her legs down with his knee and proceeded to undo his pants with his one free hand. It didn't take her long to realise she couldn't overpower him. Millie closed her eyes as tightly as she could and started counting in her head, she needed something to focus on, she thought to herself.

1, 2, 3...He pulled her pants down to her ankles... 4, 5, 6...The stink of his breath as he got close to her face, his body weight taking her breath away but she continued counting...7, 8, 9, 10...Millie tried to scream as Mr. Man of the week entered her. 11... Maybe her mom would come home early, 12... Maybe Danny would pop over to visit. 13... Please make him stop! Millie had counted to 47 when he finally got off her. She cradled her knees into her chest and scooted back to the corner of the bed. He did up his pants and left without a word. Mills ran straight to her door and locked it; she then turned the shower on as hot as she thought she could handle. Steam filled the room, but Millie just stood there crying. Her skin felt like it was melting off, but she didn't care, she sat down in the shower, letting the hot water run down her face. She cried for what felt like forever.

Eventually Millie was able to change her bedsheets, nearly gagging at the semen and blood stains left behind. She was pretty sore between her legs, and she knew the blood on the bed was hers. Mills crawled into bed and cried herself to sleep. Her mother came home a few hours later, happily humming to herself, after all she had won two games that night and her pockets were lined with an extra $40.

A few days later, her mom, none the wiser of what happened that night suggested they go visit Millie's sister Sarah. "Yea." Millie agreed, she loved going to see Sarah and her nephew Mitchell. Sarah had broken up with Mitchell's dad, but she was in a new relationship now and only lived a few blocks away.

They walked out the door, listening to her mom go on about winning the $40. As a treat they stopped at the store to buy a chocolate bar and of course her mom spent $20 of her winnings on Nevada tickets. Nevada tickets were these cardboard kind of rip open things where of course you could win money. She didn't win anything that time, but at least they enjoyed a mars bar on the way to Sarah's house.

The kettle was put on and mom and Sarah chatted away in the kitchen, Millie was holding onto the kitchen chair with one hand and the countertop with the other. She started swinging her legs back and forth. "What are you doing?" Her sister questioned her laughing. Sarah was watching Millie's legs getting higher and higher off the ground. Before she could say anything else, Millie's hands slipped. Her knee bashed into the floor before her chest hit, knocking the wind out of her. Everything went dark!

"My knee!" Millie screamed when she regained consciousness, but no actual sound came out of her mouth, she was gasping for air. Her sister was holding her on her lap and her mom was on the phone asking Millie's dad to come take her to the hospital.

Just a few minutes later, her dad ran in the house asking what the heck happened. It was just a stupid accident, but Mills didn't want her dad to blame anyone. He did get angry quickly and she really didn't want her mom in the crossfire. She mustered up the words, "I fell."

Her mom got Millie's shoes and placed them on her feet, while Sarah explained what had happened. With everyone's help Millie managed to get into the car. Her dad drove off, with Millie still clutching her knee and complaining her chest hurt.

The doctor told the two of them that Millie had knocked herself out when her chest and head hit the floor. But the worst injury she suffered was to her left knee. She needed an mri (magnetic resonance imaging) to determine exactly what damage she had done.

Her dad went to get a coffee to wait out the 45-minute scan. The radiographer placed headphones over Millie's ears, strapped her leg down and away she went, inside this huge donut tube machine. The humming and whirring sound, although it was loud, was kind of relaxing at the same time and Millie felt herself in a daydream state.

Her beautiful blonde hair was blowing in the breeze, she could smell the freshness of the crisp air. Millie's favourite place to be was outside, among the trees or by the river. In her dreamlike state, she felt beautiful, she was laughing, not a care in the world. She didn't allow the memories of what had happened to her get in the way of this dream. Here in this moment, she was free, safe and happy. She vowed to make this a reality and that one day she would experience a life like this. The corners of her mouth began to rise, and Millie completely forgot the pain she was in. She was free! No one was hurting her, no one humiliating her, she wasn't struggling for food or watching fist fights between her parents. For 45 minutes she relaxed into the humming and lived her freedom.

"Millie has crushed the patella," (knee cap), the doctor informed them. The injury was extremely serious and would most likely impair her for years to come. She was given the world's biggest needle right into her knee, a cortisone injection apparently. Millie screamed in pain.
"Jump down off the bed when you're ready," the doctor said to Millie as he walked out of the room.

"Jump down, is he out of his mind, my knee is on fire!" Millie's dad lifted her down from the table and helped her into the next room, following the doctor.

The doctor gave her a brace and crutches that she would need to use for the next 6 months, and they were sent on their way.

When Millie returned home, her dad helped her up the stairs to her mom's apartment then he turned around and left. Millie used to key to get in and shouted for her mom. There was no answer. Mills made her way to her bedroom and when she opened the door, there, on her bed, was her mother and some man she had never seen before. "This is my room!" She screamed. Millie slammed the door and ran back outside hoping to catch her dad. To her luck, her dad had decided to have a cigarette before driving off.

"Can I stay with you dad?" Millie didn't want to go back to her mom's apartment. She knew she had to leave, or she was never going to have that feeling she had in her daydream. Her dad looked at her brushing her hair from her face, he nodded. Millie didn't tell him about what she had seen, she was tired of it all and just wanted to get away. "Thanks." Mills let a small smile form on her face. He didn't question why Mills suddenly wanted to leave her mom, but he wasn't complaining either. He had missed her, and life was getting very lonely for him.

For the first couple of weeks Millie found it hard to cope. She was in pain with her knee most of the time and was pretty much stuck in the house. The good news at least was that she was with her dad and there were no more strange men coming around to 'introduce' themselves.

Paula came over almost every day to see how Millie was and always made her smile to forget her pain, at least for a little while. They would talk about boys or do homework together. Millie's other friend Katie came over quite often as well. Her older brother was actually the father of Mitchell, Millie's sister's son, so in a strange way they were sort of related, if sharing a nephew makes you related. The three girls became nearly inseparable during the time of Millie's recovery and even more so once the brace was off and Millie no longer needed her crutches to get around.

It had been a long 6 months, but it had also been a really good 6 months. Millie's dad always made sure the bills were paid and there was food in the frig and cupboards. They spent the evenings playing cards or watching tv. She was becoming really close to her dad, and it was nice to see him in a new light.

There was no mistaking how much her father missed her mom, but there was a very positive change to his behaviour. It was difficult for Millie, and even more so for her dad, when they thought about how her mom had taken them and left, but in the end her father definitely was a better person now. He had moved into a new apartment and although it was small, it served its purpose and Millie, no matter how small it was, felt very comfortable and safe. No more worries of creepy Mr. Ward or visits form Mr. Man of the week.

Her dad had lovely neighbours as well and sometimes Millie would sit on the porch and share a cold drink with them in the sunshine, The wife and son had a medical issue, though Millie never asked exactly what it was. The wife was confined to a wheelchair and the son had learning disabilities and would eventually be wheelchair bound as well. Jerry had the softest of hearts and Millie thought he was an absolutely brilliant human for taking such good care of his challenging family.

Eventually Millie and her friends started getting boyfriends and going to parties. A lot of the kids her age were drinking but Mills wasn't a fan of alcohol, even though at 16 most of her friends were. One party in particular was held at a boy's house that

Millie had a crush on, she drank the punch that night, assuming it was the best choice. Little did she know the punch was full of alcohol and Millie soon became more drunk than most of the kids around her. Within a couple of hours Millie and Paula were using the front lawn as a toilet while falling over each other and laughing about what plants were safe to use as toilet paper.

Mills had definitely drank too much. When she could no longer hold it down, seven cups of red punch found its way back up her throat and all over her brand-new sweater. The one she had bought with her wages from her two jobs.

Millie's crush offered her a clean shirt, (throwing up and her crush seeing it, was probably Millie's most embarrassing moment). Her night was over after that. She asked Katie if her boyfriend would give her a ride home, as he had been the one to take them there. Her crush offered instead and Millie, feeling embarrassed accepted. She just wanted to go to bed. Jamie drove a little way then stopped the car. He leaned over to kiss Millie and she hesitated. Putting his hand between her legs, he forcibly pressed his lips to hers. He pushed his fingers into her. Mills was a bit foggy brained and didn't completely understand what was happening. He pushed a button beside Millie's seat and she found herself almost lying down. Jamie removed her underpants and undid his zipper. He climbed on top of her and entered her right there on the side of the road, in the passenger seat of his car. Millie had imagined having sex with Jamie on more than one occasion, but not like this. It would be over soon and he would get her back to her house after he was done. She wondered, even in her drunken state was sex what it was all about? Is that what all men really wanted? As soon as she arrived safely home, her phone rang. Katie was already ringing her telling her to come back. She couldn't go back even if she wanted to, her body was definitely not happy with the amount of alcohol she had consumed. She ended up falling onto her bed and was asleep within minutes, her clothes on, although a bit disheveled.

When Mills turned 18 and finished high school, she didn't really know what she intended to do, some of her friends were going off to college but that wasn't an option for her. With her mother's gambling problem and her father just getting by, there just wasn't any extra money for further education.

That summer Millie was looking for a better job, she wasn't tired of babysitting, besides at 18 she wanted something that paid a lot better. When she wasn't working and had free time, she would sit on the porch with her dad or the neighbours and watch people going by. The best thing about living in a small-town like Welling, was everyone knew everyone. She loved having random conversations with everyone who walked by.

"Who is that?" Millie asked Jerry as they sat having coffee one morning. She gestured to a man across the street who was helping a small child out of the backseat of his car.

"Not sure," Jerry replied, "He only moved in a few weeks ago, keeps to himself mostly."

Millie was interested in finding out who this stranger was. He looked older than her, which must have been the case if the small girl was his daughter, she looked around 4 or 5 years old. Cute kid though, curly brown hair and she was always jumping around laughing. Millie wished she had felt that happy as a child, but behind closed doors anything can happen. Mills fell in love with that little girl instantly and would often think about having her own daughter one day and what it would be like to have a little hand to hold. Millie closed her eyes and imagined what she thought would be the perfect future. A husband, 2 children, maybe a dog and a little house.

Millie, not being very career oriented, felt she would be happiest being a stay-at-home mom and caring for the house and the family.

Little did Millie know that dream just might be closer than she thought. A lot closer.

Chapter 3

Marriage and her happily ever after?

Warren was the name of the man across the street and his 5-year-old daughter was Bella. Millie had watched them so often she eventually heard their names, when passer-by's addressed them to say good morning. Warren himself, had approached Millie on a few occasions asking questions about the weather or other general chitchat, Mills thought maybe he had a little crush on her.

It didn't take long and soon Warren and Millie were spending more and more time together, everything felt natural with Warren and it seemed he wasn't just after sex. They actually did stuff together, like karaoke and watching movies.

Eventually Millie was introduced properly to Bella as 'daddy's girlfriend' and they became officially a couple. In turn that meant an official 'little family.'

After a few months Warren invited Millie to move in with him. It worked out well actually as her dad was finding things difficult financially and he opted to find a bachelor apartment that would be much more affordable for him. Mills had things to collect from her mother's apartment so she decided to head over there one day when Warren was at work, it would give her an apportunity to see her mom who she hadn't seen in a few months. She knocked at the door, but no one answered, luckily Millie still had her key, so she let herself in. After gathering her personal belongings, she couldn't help but notice the state of the apartment. Millie set to work, doing the dishes, vacuuming up, and removing all the garbage. Although it wasn't perfect, she was sure her mom would appreciate what she had done. She locked up and returned to Warrens.

Over time things were going really well and Millie had landed a job with the town's small newspaper, she would be proofreading articles, developing film in the dark room, going with reporters to different events and was even given the responsibility of writing the obituary notices. Writing was probably Millie's only passion, besides having a family. It may have been the obituaries, but it was writing, and that had Millie very exciting. Bella loved being with Millie and both Warren and Bella agreed that Millie seemed a perfect fit for their little family. So much so, that on her 19th birthday Warren presented a gift of an engagement ring.

Warren had caused an argument and basically pissed Millie off, he then left the house and returned 20 minutes later with a gift. When questioning his logic with that, Warren just said it was a good way to surprise her and she wouldn't expect it.

Millie said yes but couldn't help but feel a little disappointed at how he proposed. No public display of affection, or romantic dinner for two. Jerry Springer on the tv in the background though had a first-row seat to the event. Millie tried not to show her uncertainty about the proposal, this was, in fact, a chance to start a new life.

Warren taught Millie to drive and she was able to get her licence. She would drive Warrens car when she needed to but she was excited about saving up for her own car one day.

A few months went by, and the courthouse was booked, it would be something simple and Mills had bought a cream business style dress and a jacket that would be good enough for the occasion. Only immediate family were present and the ceremony itself only took 15 minutes. They all gathered at a Chinese restaurant afterward to have a meal and celebrate.

Millie had become very good at hiding her emotions and this was no exception to the rule. This day, she needed to be happy and to smile, so she did, but inside however, she cried.

Once again Millie allowed herself to float off into her daydream state, imagining herself in a beautiful wedding gown, with a wedding party including her sister Sarah and her two best friends Paula and Katie all stood beside her. Everyone would gasp at how beautiful she looked.

Photos would be done by the river, and they would all dance the night away at the wedding reception with 200 guests present.

A tinkling of glasses brought Millie back to reality as Warren stood up to thank everyone for coming. That was it. Millie was married, she had a husband and a stepdaughter, but she just didn't feel happy.

Warren lost his job 3 months after the wedding, and it was decided they would have to move in with his parents until he was able to find another one. They had offered to let her and Warren work on their chicken farm. Mills hadn't yet learned to drive, so she had to give up her job at the newspaper, which broke her heart, she loved working there, but they needed two wages so stay on top of bills. Warrens parents however, told them they could work on the farm to earn their keep and get enough money to save up so they could move back on their own. They were given one large room in the basement to store their belongings and furniture. It would have to accommodate them as living space as well. Warren set up their bed, he placed their sofa and tv in a sort of living area so they could watch a movie or Bella could watch cartoons when she was there. all the boxes and everything else was piled up ceiling high.

Work on the farm started every morning at 5 am, and the first job of the day was to walk through all 3 barns, each holding around 200 birds, to collect the dead chickens. The process took about two hours, and Millie soon learned to wear extra layers of pants, so her legs didn't get pecked up. After she removed a total of 73 dead birds that first morning, she was able to go inside, shower and get breakfast.

Late morning the hay would come in, Millie and her father-in-law would throw the bails into the barns while Warren stacked them. Working in the barns was exhausting and the only perk, if you could call it a perk, was getting a fresh chicken for dinner every Sunday. It wasn't until that first Sunday morning that Millie realised, she would be the one to have to pluck all the feathers out, after Warren and his father chose a bird and took it out back with the axe.

As much as Millie tried to get along with her mother-in-law, they just did not click. Everything Millie did was wrong, from the way she folded clothes, to the way she peeled potatoes. Warren was being told off like a child for leaving his work clothes in the bathroom laundry hamper and Bella, when she came to stay on weekends, was told not to create too much noise or was being reprimanded for playing with the dog wrong.

"Bella, sweetie, don't pet him like that." "Bella, he doesn't like it when you chase him." "Bells, leave his ball alone, that's his favourite." Millie felt sorry for her step daughter.

One Saturday morning, while being told off for using the paper towel Millie had had enough. "Your mother is doing my fucking head in," she shouted to Warren as she walked back into their room," I can't even use a paper towel without being told off." Warren looked surprised as if he thought everything was hunky dory. Millie continued her rant, "we are moving, and we will find jobs in town, honestly I'm not staying here anymore!"

It was agreed that they would move out and luckily over the 4 months they lived there, enough money had been saved to afford a deposit on a small two-bedroom apartment. Millie had found a job working in a meat factory and Warren would be travelling to another town to work in a department store.

Moving day came and it took Millie everything she had not to hold up her middle finger at her mother-in-law as they drove away.

They lived in the apartment for about a year until an opportunity came up for Warren to become self employed as a window cleaner and garden maintenance man. They jumped at the opportunity as it meant Millie could work from home taking care of the finance side of the business. Warrens friend also set them up in a 3-bedroom townhouse in the same area where he lived. It was affordable and had office space in the basement perfect for the business.

Millie was wanting to try for a baby. Sarah had gotten married and had just given birth to a beautiful baby girl, Nellie. Holding Nellie in her arms, Millie knew she needed the same in her life. She wanted to be a mother more than anything, and although she was a part time mom to Bella, she wanted that experience for herself of being pregnant, giving birth and holding her first child.

"I'm sorry Millie," the doctor reached for her hand," it seems your body isn't ovulating like it should." Although Millie felt devastated, the doctor assured her they could try medication that would stimulate ovulation. A small dose of Clomithene citrate for the first 3 months, then increasing the dose if it hadn't worked. Mills left feeling hopeful.

Three months went by ever so slowly as Millie took a pregnancy test every time her period was due hoping to see those two pink lines. Each month she was disappointed. As agreed, another appointment was made with her doctor and her prescription was doubled. The first month, on the higher dose, when Millie took a test, she couldn't believe her eyes, 2 pink lines. Millie was pregnant, she would be 22 years old when her baby was born. She was confident she would be the best mother she could be to her new baby girl or boy.

At 20 weeks Millie had a scan just to be sure she was only carrying one child as the medication could easily cause multiple births. They were relieved to see there was only one baby present. Twins would be awesome, Millie's father was a twin with her Aunt, it would also be a lot of work for Millie to cope with.
"Do you want to know the sex of the baby?" The scenographer covered the ultrasound screen and smiled. Warren nodded and Millie agreed so it was official, they were having a girl!

Nine months went by so quickly and baby girl was wanting to make her appearance. Millie struggled to get some sleep that might. Tiny twinges of pain were making it uncomfortable enough to keep her awake. She got out of bed at 1am and decided to have a soak in the bath. After her fingers started to wrinkle up she let the water out and went downstairs to make herself a coffee. She grabbed a pen and paper to write down each time the pains came and went. By 4 am Millie had noticed the pains were about every 10 minutes apart. After trying to wake Warren, she decided to ring Sarah for some advice.

"Is Warren awake?" Sarah asked.

"No, he's been asleep all night, I just tried to wake him, and he told me to piss off." Millie was holding back the tears. "I'm scared."

Sarah instructed her to ring the doctors as soon as the contractions were 7 minutes apart or if her water broke, whichever happened first. She assured her little sister everything would be ok and hung up the phone.

Another hour passed and Millie, this time was insistent that Warren get his ass out of bed. She hadn't slept all night, she was afraid, exhausted and now she was angry at Mr. Sleeping beauty! "Get the fuck up!" She yelled.

After a gruelling labour, an emergency ambulance ride to a bigger hospital and an unexpected Cesarian section, their baby girl was born, Erica was a beautiful, chubby, healthy baby girl. Millie was pretty drowsy and knew her recovery would take a few weeks, but she also knew it was all worth it.

Bella would be so excited to meet her baby sister and Mills was sure she would be a wonderful help when she was with them. Warred picked Bells up and brought her in to see her baby sister. Her smile grew as she held Erica, she kissed the baby's forehead and rocked her in her arms. "I'll be the best big sister, I promise." Bella whispered to the baby.

Once home it only took a few days to get into a routine, or as much of a routine as possible with a newborn. Millie took to motherhood like a pro and Warren helped where he could, if he felt like it. Bella was a very proud big sister and when she was with them, she stayed within a few inches of the baby, always wanting to help.

"Alright," Warren shouted as he came home noticing Erica in Millie's arms. "Are you ever going to put that baby down, or is this how it's going to be from now on?" He obviously felt jealous, which Millie couldn't really understand.

"She's a little fussy, that's all," Millie responded. She found it easier to hold Erica rather than continually lifting her in and out of her bassinette. Her stomach still hadn't completely healed from the c-section.

Warren huffed and walked down the stairs to the office in the basement. Mills continued trying to settle Erica as well as getting dinner ready. It was difficult enough caring for a baby while staples were still in your stomach, but trying to keep up with the housework, cooking and looking after a 7-year-old was becoming more than Millie could handle. There was no use asking Warren to help, lately he had been quite happy to explain that he worked full time, the home and children were Millie's responsibility. "You wanted a baby!" She heard his voice echo in her ears.

After Erica's first birthday Millie started having dizzy spells. Unsure of what could be wrong, she made an appointment with her family doctor.

"Congratulations!" The doctor confirmed a positive pregnancy after doing a blood test. Millie was shocked as she didn't believe it would be possible to get pregnant without the help of the fertility medicine. The doctor confirmed that sometimes a healthy pregnancy can stimulate the body to correct itself. Which of course it must have done.

Telling Warren made her really nervous; he was getting more and more annoyed lately at not being the only one receiving Millie's attention. He hated when the house wasn't spotless and to top it off Erica had just started sleeping through the night.

"Oh, that's just great." Warren snapped, being sarcastic and angry at the same time. He turned and retreated to his man cave (the office). "Call me when dinner is ready!" He shouted as he walked down the stairs. Millie sighed and let out a deep breath.

The amount of time Warren was spending in the office started to raisle Millies suspicion. A little investigation soon uncovered a secret, which could be an answer to his sudden outbursts. Millie found a file on the computer with images of a naked Warren. He had sent photos of himself to different women he had been speaking to. At this point in her marriage, she didn't have the energy to mention it.

The daily routine was hard for Millie, she had to do all the housework, cooking, caring for Erica and Bella, if she was there, and now she was pregnant.

When baby number two made his appearance, they named him Jason. His birth, thankfully was a normal one and Millie didn't have to undergo a c-section this time. Mills was home the next day and recovered very quickly. Jason was a sweet baby and existed only to eat and sleep. It was a welcome adjustment for Millie, two babies can be difficult but Jason, being such an easy baby made it more enjoyable than stressful.

Warren was getting more and more desperate for Millie's attention once baby number two arrived. A few days after baby Jason was born, Warren came to bed, only after having his nightly beer and cigarette. He leaned over to kiss Millie. Mills asked Warren if he would mind brushing his teeth. She was still affected at times by what had happened to her in the past and beer breath would make her feel very uncomfortable.

"I'm horny," Warren replied, refusing to get out of the bed.

"I've just a had a baby, I'm still very sore and my God Warren, I'm exhausted." Millie snapped back without meaning to, she was tired, and her feelings were never taken into consideration when it came to Warren wanting sex.

Millie immediately regretted raising her voice. Warrens angry spiked and he grabbed her arms and pinned them down. Sitting on top of her now, his face inches from hers, he screamed!
"I'm your fucking husband and we will fuck when I say we will fuck!"

A tear fell from Millie's eyes, and she began to count. 1. 2. 3...

Chapter 4

The trials and tribulations of leaving

Millie didn't sleep that night. She waited until Warren had rolled over and started snoring, she then grabbed the baby monitors and headed downstairs. In a sort of daze, she made herself a coffee and sat with her elbows on her knees and her head in her hands. Memories of her childhood came flooding back. "Why?" She asked herself . She wondered if this seriously was how every man behaved. Millie was a sweet, kind and generous person. She knew in her heart she didn't deserve to be treated like this.

While Warren slept, Millie decided she wasn't going to take it anymore, Erica and Jason deserved a safe home. Considering her options of where they could go, she rang Sarah.

The conversation was deep and luckily Sarah didn't mind being woken in the middle of the night.

"Look Mills," she sounded very concerned about her baby sister. "Mom is in a different apartment now. There's no more men popping around all the time. She has an extra bedroom. It might be worth giving her a call." Hanging up the phone and really considering what her sister had said, Millie decided to ask if they could stay with her mother, it would only be for a little while. She would contact the benefit office as soon as they got settled. She'd get some help so she could get her own place for her and the children.

She hung up the phone from the call to her sister and rang her mom.

Millies mom, first of all, thanked her for cleaning the apartment that day. "When I walked in, I knew it was you that had tidied up for me. I took some time to think and realised how stupid I had been. I'm sorry Mills. It's better now, I promise. Bring the kids and come stay with me."

6am rolled around and Mills immediately started getting the children's bags packed. Warren, getting out of the shower seemed to have no idea or care about what he had done the night before. "What's all the fuss about?" He questioned Millie's movements as she hurried from room to room.

"I'm getting the children's things together," Millie replied in passing.

"What the actual fuck?" Warren was starting to lose his shit, but Millie was done, and she hadn't slept all night. "You're not taking my kids anywhere!"

Millie ignored him and continued in her mission. The frustration on Warrens face grew. He picked up the phone and a few moments later he spoke. "Come get these kids!" Millie heard Warren yelling into the phone. She listened in on the conversation from the hall. "I don't care, they are costing me my marriage. She doesn't have time for me, I can't take it anymore!" Millie couldn't believe her ears, was he honestly on the phone trying to get someone to take away the children? Mills stormed into the bedroom.

"I'm taking the kids and going to my moms!" Millie yelled, making sure whoever was on the phone would hear what she said, and that her children were not on offer. She took the bags downstairs and went up to get the children. Millie grabbed Jason as Erica was in bed watching cartoons. She placed Jason in his playpen and went back up to get Erica.

At the bottom of the stairs, she noticed Warren stood in the hallway between the living room and kitchen, he was holding the baby. Setting Erica down, she asked Warren to hand over the baby. "I'm taking the kids, and we are leaving, give Jason to me, I need to get him in the car."
Warren shook his head; he was quick to inform Millie that he had instructed Children services to come and collect the children.
"No one is taking my babies!" Millie screamed.

Warren reacted...

Before Millie even had a chance to brace herself, a fist flew up, hitting her on her left cheek. Millie tried desperately to get the baby away from Warren, her face now beginning to throb. She stopped thinking and instinctively reacted. Years of abuse came flooding back and Millie had completely lost it! A knife, she wanted a knife, ready to fight and this time win! 'I'll slit his fucking throat' she thought to herself, no one is taking my babies away, and no one is going to hurt me anymore! Her mind had a mind of its own now and there was nothing even Millie could do now to stop it. She lunged forward pushing herself between Warren and the wall.

Unable to get around him without jeopardising Jason, she screamed in Warrens face. "Give me my baby!"

No matter how insane Millie felt at that moment, she would not put her child in danger, maybe she was able to stop it, or maybe at the moment she

just didn't want to. Warren better be happy the children were there. Millie would have been leaving in handcuffs with a life sentence if they weren't, and she would have would have been taken away to prison with a smile on her face.

Millie stopped, looked him dead in the eyes.

"You have two choices, give me my baby, drive us to my moms and leave us the fuck alone, or I phone the police right now, they take you away for physical abuse, I then leave and take my babies." Her eyes narrowed; she was not fucking around. "Either way, you lose!"

Warren returned her glare, pushed Jason into her arms and walked out the front door. Millie heard the car start so she grabbed her bags, held Erica's hand and they walked out to get into the car.

The journey took 20 minutes and Warren never said a word. When they pulled up outside the house, Millie's mom was waiting for them. Taking the children out of the car, she handed Jason to her mom to grab the bags.

Warren grabbed her hand, "I'll get you," he whispered. Millie pulled her hand away, grabbed Erica and barely stepped away from the car when he drove off, tires squealing in a puff of smoke.

A few hours later, when Jason was down for nap and Erica was busy playing with her play dough, Millie explained a little of what happened, leaving out the details she didn't want her mother, or anyone, to know. Her mom reached over and hugged her tight. "Mills, I'm so sorry I wasn't a good mom to you, I screwed up and I don't even deserve to be forgiven, but I love you and I wanted you to know how sorry I am." Millie knew how sincere her mother's apology was, so she returned the hug and they both had a little cry.

Later that evening, Millie put Jason down to sleep in the playpen she had taken from the house, she placed Millie in bed with her. It was a tight squeeze, all 3 of them in one room, but they were safe! The phone rang around 10 pm just as Millie had been able to start dozing off.

"Bella?" Millie knew right away it was her now 9-year-old stepdaughter on the phone.

Bella sobbed into the phone, "dad won't wake up."

Millie told Bella she would call Pops (Millie's father) and have him go check on Warren and make sure Bella was safe.

"Pops will be there in 10 minutes Bells, I'll call him right away," Millie continued, "just sit on the sofa and wait for Pops ok?"

After 20 mins, when Millie was starting to get a little worried, her phone rang again. "Dad?"

Millie's dad told her exactly what had happened. Warren had picked Bella up from her mothers, when they got back home, she had asked to go play at a friends house across the street. An hour or so later Bella had come back and yelled for her dad, but he didn't answer. When she went upstairs, she found her dad collapsed over the side of the bed. Pills were scattered on the bed and a bottle of alcohol was open on the end table. Millie's dad

58

(pops) had arrived and rang the ambulance. Poor Bella was so shook up, Millie's dad was going now to drop her off back to her moms house. He told Millie He would have to drop by and pick Millie up as the paramedics had asked for his personal belongings to be taken into hospital as soon as possible.

Millie asked her mom to watch the kids and she went outside to meet her dad. She was going purely on adrenaline at this point. It felt like forever since she had actually slept more than a few minutes.

Millie and her dad went around with a duffel bag and collected some clothes for Warren, along with his personal items. While there, Millie grabbed a few more of her and the children's belongings.

If Warren had done this as a cry for help, he can keep crying. It wasn't going to work. Not today, not ever!

She stopped in the kitchen beside the block of knives. She knew if she had been able to get past him, she would have killed him. It terrified her.

Mills grabbed more bottles and formula for the baby and left.

On the way to the hospital Millie thought about how she had completely lost control at the house that morning. Abused women have killed their partners before to protect themselves. Years of abuse can totally fuck with your mind. She thought about Warrens suicide attempt and how if he had succeeded, she would then be responsible to explain it all to the children. She stopped herself from thinking about that. Warren was alive, he was an asshole, but he was alive.

 They walked in to see Warren hooked up to a bunch of wires and beeping machines. The nurse informed them he was ok but had to have his stomach pumped to remove all the pills he had taken. Leaving his bag on the chair, Millie turned to walk away. She didn't love him anymore and she was tired of pretending.

"Dad, Thanks for helping out so much tonight, but I'm ready to go if that's ok."

They made the journey back to Millie's moms, stopping for a quick coffee on the way, thanks goodness there was a 24 hour Tim Hortons close to Welling. Mills explained to her father what had happened that morning, again leaving out things she didn't really want to say. Millie never told anyone about the abuse she suffered in her life, even at that moment. She told her dad they fought all the time and even with the bruise on her cheek, she never said it was Warren who had hit her. Some things just couldn't be talked about. She didn't know why; she just wasn't able to make her lips for the word RAPE!

After achieving maybe 2 hours sleep, Millie was awakened by Erica asking to play. Although extremely tired Millie made sure to make every moment special from now on. She let the last 48 hours disappear from her mind. Cereal and Barbie's it is.

Once Mills, her mom and the kids were all awake, dressed and ready for the day, the next step was getting to the benefits office so Millie could get some help. Hopefully she could find a job eventually but first she had to get help financially and find a better place for her and the kids to live.

Two weeks passed without a word from Warren, surely, he must've been out of the hospital by now. Even Bella hadn't heard from him. Millie tried to make sure she kept in contact with Bella, after all she had been in her life for the past 5 years.

"Mills, there's a letter here for you," her mom called from the kitchen. It was handwritten across the envelope ..to the bitch my kids call mother. Warren!

Millie opened the envelope, and it was a letter addressed to Warren from the children's services, it read... In regard to your phone call...

The letter had given recognition to the request Warren made to have the children removed from the home, as well as his recent suicide attempt. He was instructed that they could not remove children from their mother's care unless there was a valid reason to do so and that Warren, because of his suicide attempt, would now have to undergo a mental health assessment and provide proof before he would be allowed contact with his children.

In huge block letters written in black marker across the letter, Warren wrote. THIS IS YOUR FAULT BITCH! I HOPE YOU DIE!

This wasn't the only letter Millie would receive, in fact she received 3 more over the next few weeks. In one envelope were 5 pages of name calling, accusations and pure disgusting verbal abuse. Millie read one particular sentence that had her immediately get her things together and go to the court office to initiate a restraining order.

"I've thought of coming after you with a gun, watch your back!

Chapter 5

Long distance

    Millie and the kids were finally settled into their own home. It had been nearly a year that her and the children had stayed with Millie's mom. There hadn't been any contact with Warren, no child support payments either. Mills was making it work with what she had. The children were happy and finally felt free, that's all that mattered. The house they moved into was split into two apartments. Millie and the children lived in the back half. It was a two bedroom, so the children had to share a room, but they also had use of the basement and a backyard to play in. Being a single mother was a lot of work, but nothing compared to what Millie had already been through, living with Warren.

The next two years Millie focused solely on the children. She took them to the park, would meet with her dad regularly for coffee at their favourite family restaurant on the Main Street and she would call or visit her mom, sister and brother whenever she could. Paula and Katie had both gotten married and Katie now had two children of her own. The world around them was changing so fast. Erica was getting ready to start junior kindergarten. She would be attending the same school Millie had gone to herself, and was such a social butterfly, she just couldn't wait to make tons of new friends. Jason had just turned 3. He really was the sweetest boy who loved cuddles and kisses. He cried when it rained and did not like his hands getting dirty.

Millie was able to save enough money to buy a computer for their little family. The kids would play games, Putt Putt saves the Zoo, was Erica's favourite. Millie used it to organise bills and listen to music. She soon discovered how to chat to people using yahoo or comic chat, which was one of Millie's favourite chat programs. Mills started running a few of the chat rooms herself while the kids were asleep, she would host karaoke and matchmaking events online. Amongst the people Millie chatted to online she had a favourite. Ted was from the UK and Mills and Ted were chatting on a daily basis.

"Good morning beautiful, " Ted posted his first message of the day.

"Hey, handsome." Millie was getting butterfime he came online.

Ted lived in a city called Hampstead and had two children of his own, he was divorced and had a very high paying job managing a company, though Millie never quite understood exactly what it was. They exchanged phone numbers and spoke on the phone very frequently.

After being in contact for 3 months, they discussed the idea of Ted flying over to Canada to meet Millie in person.

"Flight booked, leaving the Uk at 8pm your time, I'll be arriving early in the morning, so try to get some sleep." Millie was so excited to hear from Ted, and that he was going to be coming to see her,

"Can't wait!"

It was the longest night of Millie's life, excitement wise. Ted boarded the plane, on an 8 hour flight across the ocean. Millie couldn't help but feel like the most loved person in the world. A man was willing to fly across the ocean just to see her! Mills didn't have a car so she couldn't even collect him from the airport, she just had to lay in bed watching the hours go by. Ted would soon be pulling in the driveway in a rental car, but the clock ticked by, even slower when she thought of seeing him face to face.

The morning came and Millie had managed to doze off for a couple of hours at least, but knowing he would have landed and been on his way to her house filled Millie's stomach with butterflies.

Mills had the kids awake and dressed fairly quickly so she could take them to her moms for the day, she wanted to meet Ted first on their own. They had already planned that later on in the day they would take the kids on a picnic at the park. This felt like a good way to introduce them to mommy's new 'friend'.

With the kids away and the house tidied up, Millie paced back and forth, more nervous than she had ever felt in her entire life. She already knew she loved this man, even without the ability to touch him.

Months of just talking gives you an opportunity to learn everything about someone, besides that, he was gorgeous. His brown hair fell gently over his forehead, his gorgeous blue eyes and the cute little freckle like dot he had on his lip. Of course, he also had that sexy English accent.

The car pulled up in the driveway and Millie couldn't contain herself, she ran out to the car and was ready to hug and kiss him before he had even undone his seatbelt. When they embraced, Millie felt safe, his lips were like soft cotton candy and seemed to melt into hers.

They took his bags into her house and Millie showed him around her small home. Laughing and talking, they unpacked his bags and packed a picnic to have with the children.
Erica and Jason took to Ted like a duck to water, Millie couldn't be happier, she could only hope this was in fact her Prince Charming that she had hoped for. Maybe, just maybe, now , she could have her happily ever after.

9/11 had happened just prior to Teds visit, it caused a delay with his flight and he was really nervous about boarding the plane. The fact that he had come made Millie love him even more.

Sept 11th 2001, at the moment the first plane hit, Millie had been walking with the children to the park. Ted rang her and told her to get home and put on the news. For the rest of the day Millie was glued to the television. Such a horrific event, it impacted the entire world. Flights had been cancelled or delayed. Teds flight was moved forward a few days but even if it had been cancelled, Millie knew they would find a way to each other. A love like theirs would always find a way.

Two weeks went by way too fast, Ted was needing to catch his flight back to the UK. He hugged the children and promised to be back very soon. Mills couldn't help but cry, however, Ted wiped the tears from her cheeks, "I'll be back soon, I promise."

Once Ted drove away, Millie was determined to get her passport and ones for the children so they could go visit Ted in England. Little did she know, that would be a longer battle than she could have imagined.

Warren was their father, he was named on the birth certificate so she would need his permission to obtain their passports. She reached out to him, knowing the answer before she even asked but she had to try. Millie now had to figure out a way around having Warrens permission.

Ted visited again only 3 weeks later, this time he had agreed to stay for a whole month. Millie knew he had children of his own and being away from them must have been difficult. It was a sacrifice they both would have to make, in the short term, if they wanted to figure out a way to be together one day.

One of Millie's favourite memories was when Ted , grabbing a cardboard box and a hot glue gun, decided to make Jason a garage with a curved ramp, to use when he played with his toy cars. Seeing them work together was so heartwarming.

Ted was a type of celebrity in the tiny town of Welling. Everyone was excited to meet the infamous English man who had won Millie's heart.

Intimacy with Ted was on another level, when Ted touched her, it was like fireworks in her chest, he made love like Mill was the most beautiful woman on the planet. The pleasure she received from him made her forget that she had ever had sex, or that it even existed before he came into her life. This was making love.

Millie had never even experienced an orgasm but Ted made her feel like her eyes were popping out of her head. The warmth she felt when Ted released inside her, made her explode again in an orgasm of waves that didn't seem to end. She didn't just love this man, she was sure he was crafted in the hands of God, just for her.

Millie and Ted spoke about having a child together one day, she was quite content with the two children she already had, and Ted had two as well. Although it was a little crazy, there was something that seemed right about joining the families together with a child made from such incredible love.

Looking into how to apply for the children's passports without Warren, they discovered they would need to fight to obtain what's called a right of mobility order. This would give Mills the right to move the children out of the country without needing Warrens permission.

This would all take time and they needed to obtain a lawyer. Millie found Mr. Griep, who had plenty of experience with these types of cases. Mr. Griep informed Millie she would need to visit England before proceedings took place as no judge would agree to let her take the children somewhere she hadn't ever been before. She would need to assure the judge it was safe, and the children would have a nice place to live and be taken care of properly.

A flight was booked a few months after Ted returned to the UK for the second time. This time the flight was for Millie to travel. She arranged for her mom to have the children while she flew to Hampstead. It broke her heart to leave Erica and Jason for two weeks, but she knew without going, there was no way she would be able to take the children to live In the Uk.

England was like a new world, things couldn't be more different than her simple life back in Canada, in her tiny town of Welling. They visited London, Stonehenge and a beautiful little area called the new forest, which Millie adored. She was even able to meet Teds children, Jack and Tilly. They were very sweet kids and loved their dad very much. Millie bonded with the kids very quickly and showed them photos of Erica and Jason. Everyone seemed to be excited at the opportunity to combine this blended family and start a life together.

The two weeks flew by with Ted, they had been able to make a list of the things they would need to put in place to satisfy Mr. Griep. They had looked for homes that would be suitable for a large family, scoped out the schools around Hampstead and even contacted children's services in the UK to help support their application for the mobility order.

Exhausted from the busy hustle around England, Millie was looking forward to being back with her children. Leaving Ted broke her heart and she tried to compensate her feelings by reminding herself the next time she saw Ted it would be to put the application in to the courts.

The day before Millie flew home, she realised she hadn't had a period since before Teds last visit to Canada. She took a pregnancy test that evening so they would know the results before she left the next day.

Positive! Millie was pregnant with Teds baby. According to her calculations she would already be 7-8 weeks along already. Only having 24 hours to celebrate, they ordered a Chinese delivery and found a good movie to snuggle up to. Millie couldn't think of anything more perfect.

At the airport the next day, Jack and Tilly hugged Milly goodbye, watching Tilly shed a tear, although sad, warmed Millie's heart, "I'll be back soon," she said kissing the children on the cheek before turning to Ted. She wrapped her arms around him so tight.

"We will be together again soon, I promise," he whispered as he held her tight. Millie could not hold back her tears. " I'll be there," Ted continued, grabbing her chin, "I'll fight for you!"

Their fingers touched for a long as possible as Millie walked away.

Filling in the hour or so before she had to board the plane, Millie shopped for gifts for the children and of course she had to buy the infamous airport toblerone.

Millie had a few cramps in her tummy and decided she best use the toilet before the boarding started. To her dismay Millie was bleeding, not just a little, but a lot. Terrified she rang Ted and told him she would be needing to go straight to the hospital the moment she landed. The bleeding did not stop for the entire 7 hr flight and Millie must have been in and out of the toilet another 100 times before they finally landed.

She flew through customs and retrieved her luggage. As soon as she spotted her dad there waiting for her, she ran over to him and gave him a hug. "Dad, I need to go to the hospital, I'm losing my baby!

Chapter 6

England bound

At the hospital an ultrasound was done first. Millie could see her tiny baby's heart beating, a blood test however, confirmed the baby was not developing properly and there was no doubt Millie was going to miscarry over the next few days. The cramps and the bleeding continued for the next 48 hours.

Devastation hit when Millie passed the underdeveloped fetus in the toilets while shopping with her friend in Walmart. Millie sat on the floor by the hand dryers, she placed her knees against her chest, head in her hands and cried.

She would never hold her baby other than that moment, the moment when she saw the 1inch fetus on the toilet paper. That moment was sketched in Millie's heart and not a soul was told about that day in the toilets. It was Millie's time with her baby, the only moment she would ever have.

She swore, even as a tiny peanut size baby, she would never forget that she or he existed.

A DNC was scheduled within two weeks to be sure everything had been passed properly, as any part of the fetus or pregnancy related tissue could be dangerous for her if left inside. A blood test was done prior to the operation to confirm the lost pregnancy. Hearing the words 'not pregnant' broke Millie's heart. Her dad showed up the hospital and held her hand when she heard the words, "I'm sorry hun but we're going to take you now, the pregnancy test was negative so we are cleared to do the DNC."
Her father watched them wheel her away and the tears rolled down her cheeks.

It didn't take long for Mills to recover physically from the ordeal, but emotionally she was a wreck. On top of this Mills had to meet with Mr. Griep and iron out all the information regarding the upcoming court date. The case would be seen in the Supreme

Court and Millie still had to meet with Child Services there in Welling as well as finding personal witnesses willing to testify on her behalf.

During all this Mills had one huge obstacle to overcome. Warren had contacted the benefits office and reported to them that Millie was receiving financial support from Ted, which she was not! Benefits had stoped her money until she could provide proof of the contrary. This left Millie with no income to pay her bills, buy groceries or support the children with anything they may need. On top of that it was November and Christmas was around the corner. Millie hadn't even started thinking about Christmas gifts with everything else going on. Now what was she going to do? Communication with the benefits office revealed that Warren had assumed Ted was paying Millie's bills and giving her money during his visits. Millie had to explain that although, yes she was in a relationship with Ted, he had not used his personal money to pay her bills, she provided her own bank statements as proof . She explained Ted covered her costs when she went to visit him but of course that's because her money had been used for her and the children's expenses as home. Satisfied with her explanation, benefits reinstated her entitlement, although it still left her a whole month with no money.

Millie noticeably upset, wondered how Warren could have the audacity to do something like this, something that could affect his own children being able to eat or have Christmas gifts. Considering he hadn't bought them a single gift for years and hadn't spent a penny of his money to help raise them.
Paula turned up at Millie's door one day with a garbage bag, inside were gifts already wrapped and ready for the children to be placed under the tree. Millie's mother popped by with 3 bags of groceries to feed her and the children for the month and her father followed suit, giving Millie enough money to cover her rent and bills for November. Never in her life was Millie so thankful for the people she loved. It broke her heart that one day she would be moving 3,000 miles away from them.

Millie and Ted decided the best course of action to get a visa for Mills and the children would be to do so with a fiancé visa. This meant they would need to be married within 6 months of arriving in the UK, it was however, the fastest and easiest option. It all, however had to be timed properly, the visa, the court case and passports for the children.

Applications for the visa were posted out and Millie gathered the information she needed for court. Ted arranged his next flight so he could be there for the court proceedings and Millie was trying to deal with her miscarriage, as well as making sure Warren didn't try anymore of his antics.

Finally after months of hard work, the date for the court hearing was coming up. Ted came over as promised and they prepared to the best of their ability.

They booked a motel near the Supreme Court, booking 2 rooms so Millie's mother could stay with the children there while Ted and Mills attending court.

Court day 1.

Mr. Griep addressed the court on Millie's behalf . "Millie has requested to obtain a right of mobility order, to have the children placed solely in her care so that she may relocate to England. Her new partner has signed an affidavit to verify he is planning to marry Millie and that he will be financially responsible for them during the period of their visas." Mr.Griep continued. " Millie is currently unable to apply for the children's passports as their father, Warren, has refused to sign the application forms. He has not seen nor paid for the children since their separation, almost 4 years ago, Warren has since, repeatedly, sent harassing letters to Millie and a restraining order was put in place because of his threats."

After the opening statements were made a few different witnesses were called. First, the children's services, who verified Warren had not attended any of the mental health or anger management classes they had recommended, because of this Warren knew he would not be able to see the children, he still, however, chooses not to take part in these free classes.

Next was the Doctor, who verified Warrens suicide attempt, using alcohol and medication. As well as the fact that he was discovered by his then 9-year-old daughter who was in his care at that moment.

The children support worker, who represented Erica and Jason also made a statement in regards to the children's best interests. She verified how happy the children were and that they spoke extremely highly of Ted. Jason does not remember his father and Erica has a fear of Warrens anger.

After hearing what the children had gone through and taking into deep consideration the abuse Mills had suffered, along with Warrens mental state, it was becoming very favourable for Millie. After everything had been adjourned for the day, they made their way back to the hotel. The heavens had opened up and it was raining fairly heavily. Millie feeling extremely confident on how things were going, took off her shoes and started dancing in the rain, outside their hotel room. Ted and the children joined in while Millie's mom watched from the window. She could tell by her moms expression that she thought mills had gone bonkers.

Court day 2

This was the day Warrens side had the chance to rebuttal some of the things mentioned the day before. After a brief opening statement, Warrens lawyer, being pressured by Warren himself, spoke hesitantly. " Your honour, my client would like to mention that yesterday it was said that he had not financially supported the children since their seperation. Warren, however, would like to make it known he had purchased a gift for his daughter." Confused looks covered everyone's faces.

"Go on," the judge replied.

" My client says the gift was a Barbie that he has kept for Erica as he believes it will be worth money in the future if it is left unopened." Warrens lawyer, obviously not happy making the statement he was being forced to make.

The judge looked Warren dead in the eyes and spoke directly to him.

"Let me get this straight, you refuse to acknowledge you need any help with your anger or mental health, because of this you basically forfeited being able to see your children. You have not provided financially for them; however, you are refusing to sign their passport applications. Your children have the opportunity to be raised by a man they obviously love. The only gift you have provided in the last 4 years, you purchased for just one of your children, and you did not intend to give the gift to her?"

Warren interrupted, "I intend to give her the Barbie when she is older..."

The judge threw his hands up, slammed his hammer down and proceeded to interrupt Warren. "The children will be placed in the sole custody of their mother, she will be granted the right of mobility order and is therefore free to relocate with the children, wherever she pleases. Case closed."

Warren still standing, lost his ever-loving mind. Curse words flew out of his mouth towards the judge, towards his lawyer and obviously towards Millie.

Ted and Millie left the courtroom while watching Warren being dragged out by two security guards. Millie thanked her lawyer and everyone else present that had helped with the case. Now it was time to get the passports and wait for the visas to be processed.
It felt wonderful when Millie returned home with Ted and the children. Ted would have to leave in a few days, he would move into a bigger house and get everything prepared for their arrival, which hopefully wouldn't take longer than a few months.

As hard as this goodbye was, they both knew it was the last goodbye. The next flight would be Millie and the children leaving, then starting their life in England with Ted.

The children's passport arrived 6 weeks later, with that Millie was then able to send them off to have the visas finalised.
Millie popped into the doctor's office after posting the information from the post office. She hadn't had her period since Ted left and wanted to be sure everything was ok.

"Pregnant, congratulations," the nurse smiled.

Millie was given a positive blood test from the nurse and she couldn't believe her eyes. She was once again pregnant with Teds child. This time she was afraid that something may go wrong again, however she picked up the phone and rang Ted to let him know.

"We need to get you over here as soon as possible," Ted said, obviously wanting to be there for her through the pregnancy. Both Millie and Ted had no idea how long the Visa process would take, it was June now and both hoped they could be in England before the start of the new school year.

August came and so did the visas! Ted booked a flight for the three of them, and it worked out that they would arrive in the UK on Aug 24th 2003. Erica would start in year 2, with Jason starting in reception. With the paperwork all in order the only thing left was the horrendous goodbyes Millie would arrange with family and friends.
Paula arranged a photoshoot so she could have final photos with her best friend before they left.
A barbeque was held at her sister Sarah's home for friends and family to gather to say their goodbyes.

They had a wonderful day full of laughter and smiles, photos were taken and memories made. However, Millie didn't realise just how long it could be before she saw her family and friends again. She tried to hold back the tears when the time came to say goodbye. Everyone there loved her unconditionally and that was something so many people have taken for granted, including Millie. On the way home Erica took it really hard, sobbing uncontrollably. "We will see everyone again really soon," Millie comforted her precious daughter.

She had to believe what she was doing was the best thing for all of them.

On August 24th Millie's dad turned up to drive them to the airport, she had made arrangements for a local auctioneer to collect everything for her home after she left. With them, they only took two large suitcases, Erica and Jason had a small suitcase of their own for their special toys.
At the airport the kid's excitement grew. It was a big day for a 6- and 4-year-old. They were having one of the biggest days of their lives and they didn't even know it.
Once the bags were all checked in, Millie's dad walked them to the gate. "I love u dad," Millie said already crying as she hugged her father.

After lots of hugs, I love yous and see you soons, they disappeared through the gate and headed toward the plane.

As the engine of the plane revved up, the kids started to laugh, nervous laughter, or excitement? More than likely both. Millie, trying to smile, but her eyes weren't fooling anyone. Her heart broke in a million pieces, "when will I see them again?" She thought as she looked out the window of the airplane, the only world she ever knew would soon disappear from under her.

Chapter 7

Broken soul

Everything started off on a bad foot, starting with the flight. They stayed stationary on the runway for 2 hours before the pilot announced there had been a major power outage. "We are waiting for the backup generators to kick in folks, then we will be on our way."

Finally after and another hour the planned revved up and started its journey. Millie was worried as they had a connecting flight in Amsterdam, surely they would miss it. The stewardess assured passengers that connecting flights would be sorted upon arrival in Amsterdam and gave them a booth number to find when they landed.

Although the flight was at night, the children stayed awake for most of it. Breakfast was brought around about an hour before the plane landed, that's when Erica and Jason finally decided to fall asleep. Millie took a juice and muffin for each of the children from the stewardess so they could eat something later and she let the children sleep.

In Amsterdam, Millie found the booth and was given a free calling card so she could ring Ted to tell him about their delay. She recieved new connecting tickets and proceeded to the gate.

With all the stress, Millie was lucky she had only experienced a little nausea from the pregnancy so far, however, she was only 2 months along, so she tried to retain her excitement for the pregnancy, just in case anything went wrong.

As the plane landed, Millie woke the kids again and even with only an hour sleep the excitement was enough to give them a new burst of energy. They gathered their belongings and Millie took down the carry-on bag from the overhead compartment.
At boarder control everything went smoothly, Millie showed them the visas and explained she was relocating to England permanently. They found their bags on the baggage reclaim, well, all except 1. Erica's bag had gone missing. Millie filed in a missing bag slip and added the new address so the bag could be brought to them when it was located. Erica was not happy but Millie was able to reassure her that it would be found soon and her toys were

just enjoying a little holiday before coming to the new house.

They then followed the crowd of passengers through the arrivals doors to waiting loved ones.

"Mills," Ted shouted as he noticed Millie and the kids coming through the doors. They all ran over to great him, Millie however happy, still felt a sadness in her heart that was hard to shake. The children fell asleep quickly in the car and slept the entire 2-hour journey back to their new home. Millie vowed to stay awake to make the transition to the time difference a little easier.

Pulling up to the house Millie woke the children, adrenaline fuelled bodies rose to the occasion. Running inside Erica couldn't wait to see her room.

Once they had a few days to settle, Ted went to bring Jack and Tilly to meet the children. They all got on really well and were off playing together like they had been friends for years. Adjusting to a family of 6 might be more difficult for Millie than it would be for the children. She had been a step mother before to Bella, but she knew Jack and Tilly were older and this was a whole new experience for them.

Millie found a family doctor for the three of them and booked an appointment straight away so she could have her pregnancy assessed to assure all was going well.

The children were going to start school within a few days so Ted and Millie took the children school shopping. They had never needed to wear a school uniform before and both seems very excited about it.Excitement wasnt the word Millie would use for how she was feel. There was so much to do so quickly and all she really wanted to do was sit on the sofa and put her feet up.

On the first day of school, Millie woke up extra early. She had a shower and got the children's lunch ready before waking them up. The school was only a 10 minute walk away so she planned to walk as it was a nice day and she wanted to have a look at the neighbourhood anyway. A park was located directly across from the school and the children were excited to play there after school everyday. Kissing them goodbye when the bell rang, Millie handed the children off to their respective teachers and made her way from the school.

She then proceeded to attend her doctor's appointment, which she was able to make just in time. Luckily most things were within walking distance, one good thing about living in the city. It was all just so different from Millie was used to.

The doctor did a scan and blood test, confirmed everything was looking good and Millie felt a mountain of relief. She was excited to get back and tell Ted . Unfortunately Ted was at work so Millie waited for him to get home. In the meantime she tidied up around the house and prepared a lasagna for dinner later,Teds favourite.

Mills left to get the children from school. "Can we play at the park?" Jason shouted as soon as he ran out the classroom door. Millie agreed and they went across the street with most of the other parents and children as well.

Once home, Mills saw Ted sitting at the computer. "You're home already?" Millie questioned walking into the dining room where Ted was sat. Very quickly Ted minimised the screen so Millie couldn't see what he had been doing. Millie lowered her eyebrows, questioning his behaviour in her mind.

"Ya, just had a bit of paperwork to finish." He left the computer on while he walked into the kitchen. Millie reached over to open the screen back up and saw an email account. The email Ted had been writing was not a business email. He was responding to a woman about a photo she had sent him. Millie closed the screen again and decided she wouldn't say anything right away. Maybe she was assuming the worst and jumping to conclusions. She couldn't let herself believe Ted was anything less than perfect.

Over the next 6 months, despite the computer incident of course, things were going well. Millie was getting bigger and preparations were put in place for the baby's arrival. Millie only had one issue, and that was the way Ted was

excruciating obvIous that his children were treated differently than Millie's.
Millie went into labour on a Sunday morning

about 5 am, she waited to wake Ted as it was still early and things hadn't progressed too quickly just yet. Jack and Tilly were with Ted this weekend and they were up getting dressed for the day. Erica and Jason came down in their pyjama's. Ted made an appearance a few moments later. Millie told him she was having labour pains and asked what was going on. "Tilly and Jack are dressed already, did I miss something?"
Ted responded, "I'm taking Jack and Tilly swimming," he kissed Milly on the cheek.

Confused Millie asked, "What about Erica and Jason?"

"Im spending time with MY kids, is that ok with you?" Ted was stern. Millie, not happy with the situation, reminded him she had just told him she was in labour.

"We will be back in a couple of hours; you won't drop the baby out before then." Did Ted not see anything wrong with this?
She took herself upstairs, determined not to let Ted see her anger, with aggression Millie turned on the faucet, smashing her thumb into the tap.
" Owww fuck!" Millie yelled, not intending to swear but unable to hold it back, Erica came running to see if her mommy was ok. Tears in her eyes from the pain as well as her anger at Ted, she sat on the side of the bath holding her thumb. Erica went to get an ice pack, playing nurse to her injured mom.

"Thanks sweetie," Millie brushed her daughters hair away from her eyes.

"Can we go swimming too?" Erica's little voice hurting Millie's heart.

" Sorry Erica, just Tilly and Jack are going today. As soon as mommy has the baby, Jason and Mommy and you will take the baby and go for a swim ok?"

Erica nodded, Millie hated this, my kids, your kids thing, Things had to change.

Ted left the house, with his kids in tow. Millie, Erica and Jason put on cartoons and had a nice pancake breakfast. She wrote down her contractions and so far they were 8-10 minutes apart. Her thumb throbbing, her anger at Ted obvious and her contractions increasing as time went by. All this made it difficult for Mills to function. Instead she sat down with her head in her hands and cried, once again. She started to wonder what was going wrong, everything with Ted was changing.

Ted and his kids came home a couple of hours later and as soon as he walked in the door Millie told him they had to go to hospital. Contractions were now 5 minutes apart and Mills was in a lot of pain.

"Just going to drop Tilly to her friends house, then I'll come back to get the rest of you." Was he really this oblivious to what he was doing?
" Ted," Millie yelled, "I need to go to the hospital, the baby is coming."

Without a word, Ted and Tilly disappeared out the door. Am I invisible? Millie wondered. What the absolute fuck?
With Erica and Jason's help, Millie got the bags for the hospital by the front door and they packed an

overnight bag for the children, just in case. Ted had arranged for his brother to have the children while they were at the hospital having the baby.

He finally returned 45 mins later. Without a word, Millie got the children into the car, barely able to walk at this point.

They left Jack, Erica and Jason with Teds brother and sister-in-law, then made the journey to the hospital. By this time, it was nearing 2 pm.
Millie was taken into a delivery room and settled. The pains were very close together now and baby was coming.
Rylie was born a few hours later, a beautiful healthy 8lb baby. All the children were very excited to meet Rylie when they brought her home from the hospital the next day. Millie h still had hope that Rylie would be the glue that would bond them all together.

The next new few years went by very well, the children grew and changed, as kids do. Teds children were now entering the teenage years, which started to make things a little more difficult though. One of the issues Millie and Ted had that she found hard to handle was the ever-changing rules between, his kids and hers.
Tilly and Jason only lived half the time with Ted, so he was always trying to save everything for when his

children came to the house. Want a takeaway for dinner, wait till Tilly and Jack come, kids want treats, wait till Tilly and Jack come, chores around the house, Erica and Jason did theirs but Tilly and Jack could do what they pleased.

Millie described herself as a ghost quite often when Teds children were there, Tilly would overlook Mills cooking dinner, then phone her father at work to ask what they were having to eat that night. They would invite friends over for dinner but not inform Millie. On many occasions Millie didn't eat dinner as her portion was needed for one of their guests.

It was a difficult time for Millie, raising Rylie, taking Erica and Jason to school, taking care of the home and walking on eggshells around Ted and his children.
She hadn't met any friends yet either so it became a very isolated life. She found herself clinging to Ted when he was around and was possibly coming off a bit smothering. That's the excuse she gave for his behaviour, the same behaviour she found out about with the computer a few years earlier but had slid it under the carpet.

Ted started hiding his phone from Millie, he would sit on the sofa but put the phone beside him in the cushions. He was texting people quite often but never telling Millie who he was conversing with.

Erica and Millie signed themselves up for a charity run one year. Millie woke early to make a good breakfast for them before they were to meet everyone else at the park. It was a 10k charity run for the heart and stroke foundation.
While cooking bacon and eggs Mills hear a phone beep, she saw Teds phone on the counter and assumed he had forgotten it downstairs. Not thinking too much about it, she picked it up. The text message he received said this, "Can't meet you at 10 but I'll be there at 10:30, love you." Love you? The text came from someone apparently called 'Dave'.

Mills wasn't stupid and too many times in her life she had let things slide, she never held people accountable for their actions. This time was different, she had given up her family, her friends and her entire life for this man and what was he doing behind closed doors? Millie was going to find out.

Throwing the phone onto the bed she woke Ted from his slumber. "Who the fuck is that?" She said, referring to the suspicious message. "Apparently, they 'love' you!"

Ted woke up, his eye wide open for someone just coming out of a deep sleep, He spent the next 5 minutes trying to deny whatever the message was, he didn't know who sent it, it must've been sent to a wrong number. He had every excuse, but the lie was staring him in the face.

Libby was someone Ted had met through work; he wasn't just cheating on Millie, but he eventually admitted he was in love with her.

Millie didn't say anything else, she turned and walked away, she woke Erica and they had a lovely breakfast then set off for the charity run. 10 km gave her plenty of time to think. She didn't know if the marriage was worth it. Marriage, the wedding was even smaller than her first one. Another simple courthouse ceremony, only two of Teds friends were present to act as witnesses.
She laughed to herself, he only married her because it was the easiest way to sort out the visa, but why bring her here to be cheated on?
Millie knew all too well how to have many different emotions at the same time, anger, sadness, humiliation, jealousy. Regardless of how she felt in those 2 hours, she was with Erica. They were doing something fun for a good cause and Millie's charitable heart wanted this to be something that

helped grow Erica into a good person.
Millie focused on her daughter and would deal with that two-timing bastard when they got home.

When the event was over and the girls returned home, nothing was said. Millie concentrated on the children and decided the conversation that needed to be had, could wait until the kids were in bed,

Tucking her babies in that night took longer than normal. She hugged them extra tight and kissed them more times than she could count, "I'm so sorry," she whispered as she walked out their door, switching off the light. "I thought we would have a happy life here."

Mills took 10 minutes in the bathroom to compose herself, she thought about Ted and the email, the hidden phone, the working late excuses. It was all adding up now. She wanted to be so angry, she wanted to hate him for what he was doing. Instead, she felt her heart break. Ted waited at the bottom of the stairs for Millie to finish with the children, his eyes looked sad. Her tears fell as she looked at his face and remembered how much she loved him. He was supposed to be her Prince Charming. Mills sat down on the sofa, again placed her head in her hands and whispered, "Why?"

"Im sorry, Mills." Ted didn't know what to say, he tried to defend himself, "I felt trapped, I didn't have any freedom, I was smothered."

Millie explained that she was in a country where she didn't know anyone, she loved him and he was her best friend, her only friend here. Ted felt trapped, but Milly was the one trapped, she was 3,000 miles from the people who loved her.
They talked for hours that night, was there any saving their marriage? Millie didn't know if she would ever trust Ted again, or if Ted even loved her and wanted her anymore. Even if he did, would she still want him?
Millie went to bed, crying herself to sleep. She didn't know when or if Ted had come to bed, maybe he stayed on the sofa that night. It just didn't matter.

Millie woke up around 4am, Ted wasn't in the bed, she looked downstairs, he wasn't there either, he was gone,

A note was left on the kitchen counter, it read...

Millie:

I'm sorry, I don't know what happened or why, all I know is I fell in love with someone else, I'm going to stay with my brother for a while to clear my head. I don't expect you to forgive me and I don't even know if I want you to. It was probably best you found out when you did. Maybe this was all a mistake.

Ted

    Millie read the letter over and over again, she picked up the phone and called her dad, like she always did when she felt sad. "Daddy, can you come over?"

Chapter 8

Finding life on our own

Without hesitation, Millie's dad booked a flight to the Uk. He was by her side within the week and Millie was so grateful. Millie and her father were both avid list makers and this would be no exception to the rule.

1. Contact social services.

Millie was working now, she had started a job at a school as a lunchtime assistant. It was only part time, so it wouldn't be enough to support herself and the children.

2. Change child benefit into Millie's name.

When they had first come the Uk, Millie was not entitled to any sort of government funding, things like child benefit were put into Teds name instead.

3. Look for a suitable home.

The house they lived in now was a 4 bedroom home and cost way more than Millie would be able to afford. She would have to move somewhere smaller and cheaper.

4. Buy a car.

Millie needed to take the advice of a new friend she had met, Lily. Lils and Millie had met a few years ago but were just recently becoming closer. Lily had told Mills that she really should think about driving. Millie had her license but hadn't even thought of driving in the Uk, everything was on the wrong side of the road or the right side? It was confusing but Lily was right.

5. Change everything out of Millie's name that she was no longer responsible for.

Ted had a phone that was in Millie's name, she had given him her contract phone so he could use it for work, but she definitely needed to either cancel the contract or have Ted change it into his name.

Millies dad was staying for two weeks and vowed to help her do as much as he could before he had to leave. Millie considered the option of just going with him. Taking her children, getting on a plane and going home. She had to face reality that it wasn't the answer, she didn't have the thousands of pounds it would cost for the flight and things were not that simple anyway. Rylie, was Teds daughter and she couldn't just take her to Canada without his consent. Millie had been there.... she had the T-shirt!
An appointment with the benefits office was made, she rang the mobile phone company but it was going to cost a few hundred pounds to get out of the contract. To switch the phone into Teds name, it was Ted who would need to call. Add that to the list.

6. Tell Ted to change the phone contract to his name.

When the children were all settled in bed one night, Millie and her dad went through the local rental properties, they made notes on the ones that could be suitable and in the price range Millie could afford.

They then made hot chocolate and just talked for hours. Millie's dad never made her feel bad for moving away, even though it was slapping her in the face that it was definitely the wrong decision. It wasn't the time for a blame game, it was a, I'm here to help you time.

After a few hours sleep, Millie was awake preparing breakfast for her children and her father. She had a few houses to ring about and see if they could get viewings. She had arranged with her job to have time off as she basically needed to figure her life out. They were very understanding and allowed Millie two weeks off.

Mills was able to get viewings for 3 different properties that day, so she and her dad walked the kids to school and made their way to the first viewing.

Of the three houses they looked at Millie decided to put in an application for a 3 bedroom home that was only a 10 minute walk to the kids school.

A few days later Millie received her benefits and was able to agree on a moving date for the new property. She spent the next few days packing up and deciding what she needed vs what she was leaving for Ted to collect once she was gone.

Millie purchased a small car, she was amazed she didn't have any issues with driving, even though it was quite alien driving on the opposite side of the road. As Millie had now lived in the Uk for 4 years she must've adjusted just by being a passenger with Ted.

As the day approached that her dad would have to fly back, Millie became terrified. She was a single mother again. She really wouldn't have anyone to help her. She had the children, and she was thankful for them, but she was scared.

Now that she at least had a car she was able to drive her father back to the airport. She couldn't thank him enough for coming to be with her when she needed him most.

As a child Mills was afraid of her dad, when he has his outbursts, she didn't like him very much.

She hugged her dad remembering one thing about him that she will never forget. Her dad never broke a promise to her. He wasn't the same man that he was all those years ago.

"I'll be back to visit soon, I promise." That's all she needed to hear.

"OK Millie," she spoke to herself as she walked away from the departures area of the airport after their final goodbyes. "Pull up your big girl pants, you got this!"

A car in the drive, a nice little house for her and the children, a part time job and everything now sorted, Millie, for the first time actually thought she might be ok. In total, Ted and Millie had been married 4 years. She gave up everything for 4 years?

One thing she had learned from all of this, she would never again move her entire life for a man.

Ted would come around and collect Rylie from time to time, he would take her out for a few hours then bring her back. He ignored the fact that Erica and Jason had called him Dad and missed him. They were not his kids and he made that very obvious. Ted had been a box of broken promises, it was taking Millie time to realise that, but every day she was getting stronger, and she was starting to see him for who he really was. It was the thrill of the catch. He loved Millie, there was no doubt in her mind, but he loved her when he didn't have her. Once she was here, everything changed. There were no holidays with the children, no date nights, no visit home to Canada. Above all of that, pretty much from the moment they arrived Ted had been engaging with other women.

Mills recalled one night, when Ted was being distant emotionally, she tried to entice him. Getting naked upstairs, she put on a hockey jersey she had purchased for him in Canada. She did her hair and make up, feeling sexy and confident she walked down the stairs. With a smile on her face, she strolled into the living room, and for just a moment Ted put down his phone. He looked up at Millie and frowned, "why are you wearing my jersey, get it off for Christs sake."

That right there, that one sentence, destroyed Millie's self esteem. She no longer felt pretty, she felt stupid for trying to be sexy. She felt broken.

It was time to make her life herself, to make it the best she could for her children. Millie knew she was strong and she would do whatever it took to make sure her kids were happy.

(Just for a moment I'd like to grab your attention to something I've read regarding single mothers and benefits. To the man who thinks it's ok to tell a single mother to "get a job," "keep her legs closed," or "stop having kids if you can't afford them." I am only one example of what single

109

mothers go through, I was married to the fathers of my children, I was abused and I was cheated on. I took care of my children everyday, I take them to school, attend parent teacher night, clean up their barf and nurse them back to health. I am their rock and I stand beside them 24/7. I work if and when I can around my responsibility to my children, They will forever be first in my life. Now let me ask you where their father is? The one who gets a pat on the back if he visits his kids or pays his child support. Big fucking woopie! He probably has no idea what their favourite food is, or the colours they like. But as single mothers it's easy to tear us down because we need to rely on benefits.

In the same respect, I applaud the dads out their visiting their children, loving their children and doing the best they can to maintain a relationship. I think we all need to stop judging books by their covers, everyone has a story and before we badmouth anyone for receiving benefits, we need to think about what they may have been through)

Millie booked a little holiday for her and the children near the beach, they spent 4 days, playing, swimming, having picnics and just enjoying each others company.

The kids loved it and Mills loved watching their smiling faces, at times however, her sadness was hard to hide. She watched couples holding hands, mothers and fathers with their children, it made Millie's heart heavy. All she ever wanted was someone who loved her. She was alone, in her own little bubble and no matter what she did there was no escaping it.

Nearly two years later Millie's dad suggest they come back to Canada to visit. He had saved up enough to pay for the plane tickets for her and the 3 children, all Millie needed to do was to save up some spending money. Sarah agreed for Mills and the kids to stay with her for the two weeks. She had a lovely big house now that 3 out of her 4 children (her children and stepchildren) had now moved out.

A few nights before they were going to fly home Millie had a nightmare that woke her with the most horrible night sweats. In her dream, Warren had found a way to stop Erica and Jason from returning to the Uk with her after their trip. She was being forced to leave but couldn't take the children back with her. They were begging her not to go while she was being pushed through the gates, onto a plane.

Instead of feeling excited to go home, Millie was terrified.

The day they were due to go home, they drove down to the airport and parked the car. Mills and the children found their gate and boarded the plane. It had been almost 7 years since they had seen their family back home. In that seven years Millie had missed out on so much. Her niece and nephews getting married. The births of their children. Her niece Nellie being diagnosed with cancer. Thank goodness Nellie was ok now, but it was horrific for a long time and Millie only wished she could have been there to help Sarah. The guilt set in again and Millie hated leaving that day to lve in the Uk. "I should've stayed," Millie thought to herself, beating herself up about the decision she had made. In one way she hated Ted for taking her away from everyone and in another, she hated herself for not realising just how important family really is. Now it was too late, she had lost nearly 7 years.
When it was time to say goodbye she knew she would lose many more years.
Millie's father collected them from the airport and the drive to her sister's house took over two hours. Everyone was exhausted, however, as soon as the

car drove up to Sarah's house, Mills flung open the car door and ran to her sister, who was standing on the porch waiting for them. Sarah ran to Millie as well and the sisters embraced.

Sarah had planned a family get together for them at her home and all of their family attended. Millie realised how alone she felt in the UK when she was there with so many people who loved her. Sarah's son Mitchell was all grown up now and Millie wept like a baby when she saw him. This severe reaction surprised her, sometimes you don't know who touches your heart the most until you are forced to be away from them. Sarah's husband put on a barbeque. They all drank, ate, laughed, danced and sang the night away. It was the most fun Millie had had in forever. The rest of the two weeks were spent visiting friends, or just relaxing at home with Sarah. Millie missed her big sister so much and as the days got closer to the time she would have to say goodbye, she found it harder and harder to think about anything else. She was thankful that Warren hadn't found any way to keep Erica and Jason in Canada, in fact he probably didn't even know they were back. Millie was confident that all three children would be going back to the UK with her. However, at this point even Millie didn't want to go back.

When she thought about it, Erica and Jason had now spent more of their lives in England than they had in Canada. Mills thought about how selfish she had been, bringing the children across seas just to be with the man she had fallen in love with. She felt guilty for taking them away from so many family members that loved them and missed them so much. They had their own lives in the UK now and going back to Canada permanently would be another selfish move she was not willing to make. When the day came for them to leave, there were more tears than drops of water in the ocean. Millie sobbed her heart out more than she had ever done before. For three months following that visit, Mills was very quiet. She took that time to reflect and to think about what she had done to get to where she was now.

Millie got a second job, she wanted to provide as best she could for her children. She took a sign language class and obtained her level 2 qualification in child care and development. Mills focused on herself, to make a better life for her little family.
Although Millie was lonely for male affection, she hadn't really thought of dating yet, she hadn't had the energy or desire to put herself out there like that, not yet anyway.

Lily became a very close friend to Millie, they saw each other a few times a week for their regular coffee mornings. After a few months, Millie told Lil she was thinking about dating again. She had downloaded a dating app and had been talking to one person, Neil, who seemed really nice and she thought it might be good to get back out there, so to speak.

Neil and Millie met at a local pub, had a drink and a chat. They laughed and everything seemed to be going really well. Mills enjoyed Neil's company immensely and over the next few months she spent almost every Friday evening with him. They never gave their relationship a title, never met each others family and never went out anywhere either. She simply went to Neil's home, had a coffee, they would talk, sometimes it would lead to sexual intimacy but that was it. Mills was beginning to feel used but she knew Neil wasn't that type of guy, he just wasn't ready to make anything official. Although she thought the world of Neil she had to walk away before she got really hurt.

It was a while before Mills dated again, and when she was ready, she found Ryan. She hadn't dated any black men before, but he was very attractive and they seemed to have a lot in common. Not understanding how it all happened, but Millie ended up in the same situation again. This time it was Sundays; Millie would spend most Sunday evenings with Ryan. They would share a meal, a drink or two, watch a movie and end up sleeping together. Eventually Millie even stayed the night and would leave at 6am on Monday mornings when Ryan got up for work. Mills would then go home and get Rylie up for school. Erica and Jason were teenagers now and happy to watch Rylie on Millie's Sunday excursions, just so they could have the house to themselves. The adventures with Ryan continued for over a year. It took Millie that long to realise she was in the exact same situation with Ryan as she had been with Neil. No relationship, no commitment, just a bit of companionship. Millie knew she needed more when her trips back to the car at 6am left her sobbing into the steering wheel. She knew she loved Neil and Ryan, but they didn't love her and that hurt Millie's heart.

All she had ever wanted was love but why was she just so unlovable?

Chapter 9

New family and friends

Although things hadn't worked out exactly the way she wanted it to with Neil or Ryan, Millie was happy they could still be friends, she was still finding her feet in the world of being a single mother. Luckily she had a few friends, some she had made from the perks of the school gates.

Millie was now going out to have coffees, meals and taking the kids to play at the park with some of the moms from school. Lily specifically continued to be a big part of Millie's life and was starting to feel more like a sister than a friend. Her husband and two sons became family and they all welcomed Millie and the children with open arms.

Although Mills still hadn't found love she had found a belonging. She wasn't so lonely anymore.

Paula and Katie kept in touch with the use of the computer, or they would exchange the odd phone call, their friendships would never die no matter how far apart they were.

Millie saw an ad one day about ancestry research and began using the computer to track down relatives. Millie's grandmother on her fathers side was adopted as a baby back in 1919. Her uncle had tried to find out some information regarding her adoption but her nana had passed away and shortly after her uncle passed away as well. Millie decided she would take over and see if she could unlock the family mystery for her dad before he passed away as well. The problem soon appeared that back in the early 1900s records of adoptions weren't always necessary. You could pretty much give up your kid to anyone at anytime. One thing Millie did get a hold of was a birth certificate. It belonged to the lady who had raised her grandmother. Millie spent hours upon hours trying to match this lady with her nana, but she found very little, according to the birth certificate, this lady was born in England in 1884. Millie's great grandfather on her fathers side was also English, arriving in Canada in

1905.

It seemed Millie bringing her children to the UK was not so alien after all, maybe she was completing a circle on the family tree.

Throughout her search, Millie was able to locate a few distant cousins that lived in England. She was pretty surprised to find out that the area her ancestors were from was only about a 30 minute drive from where Millie and the children lived. Even Kate, the woman who raised her grandmother was born only a short distance away, sometimes it really is a small world.

Over the years living in England, Millie's father visited quite a few times and even flew over one year for Christmas. Millie and the kids took pops to see London, Stonehenge and Stratford upon Avon to Shakespeare's birthplace. Most of his visits though were just time to catch up and enjoy each others company. Bella came over once as well, the children were so excited to see their sister. Erica especially loved having her big sister back and they spent every moment together. When Rylie was a baby, Millie's parents came over together, it was the one and only visit her mother would make to the UK. Millie loved that they could put their differences aside to make the trip together. She couldn't help but think of what an awkward 7 hr flight that was.

It wasn't long after that visit that Millie's mom had a stroke, her sister rang with the news.

"Mom had a major stroke Mills and while she was in hospital she had a second stroke. She's ok but there has been some permanent damage to her right side."

Millie was devastated that she couldn't be there to go see her mom herself. It did mean tho, that her mom would never make the trip to the Uk again.

Paula made the effort to fly over, she was undergoing an application for adoption and wanted to get over before that all went through . Once Paula and her husband adopted a child it would be quite some time before she would be able to come over again. Paula and Millie always picked up exactly where they left off when they did see each other and it was like being 13 again. They laughed and cried and reminisced about everything they had been through as children.

One of the most amazing visits Millie received was a surprise visit, she had no idea was coming. Arriving hom from work one day, Millie saw Erica sat on a chair with her phone pointing at her mother. Mills stopped in the doorway to open the mail and questioned Erica about what she was doing, when Millie walked around the corner into the living room, she heard a voice, "Surprise!" She knew that voice.

Millie flung around and screamed, "Fuck off! "A reaction of pure bewilderment as she would never have guessed in a million years, her sister would be sat in her living room. "What are you doing here?" Millie said between sobs. She dropped to the floor crying happy tears completely overwhelmed. This was the very best surprise Millie had ever received. Erica still holding her phone, crying, had recorded that memorable moment.

Millie always tried to remember all her amazing family and friends, every time she felt lonely. Someone wasn't always physically there but she knew she was loved. That was enough to give her the strength to make it through the tough times.

As much as she was adjusting England was not home to Millie. Canada was always going to be what she considered home.

She did soon learn though that home didn't need to be a physical place, it was when you felt in your heart that you belonged. Although her family was 3,000 miles away, Mills had someone here that made her feel home. That was her new sister Lily. Lily and her family 'adopted' Millie and her children into their family and even when Millie didn't feel at home physically, she had a 'family' here and that was home in her heart!

Devastation hit Lilys home, when her husband was diagnosed with pancreatic cancer. Her lived for 5 months with this horrible disease.
It was a difficult time for Lily and Mills made sure she was there to comfort her as much as she could.

As well, Paula has lost her brother to suicide, after he fought a battle against mental health and physical disabilities causing him tremendous pain.

Millie hadn't had to go through the emotion of someone close to her passing. She had lost her grandmother and uncles and aunts, but in her family there wasn't much contact with extended family.
At the moment, Millie's mom has the later stages of dementia, she is doing well considering but it is becoming harder and harder for her to care for herself. Sarah has taken on most of their moms care and Millie, although feeling guilty trusts her sister is doing everything she can.
Sarah, over the years has become Millie's hero. She

looks up to her in every way possible. Their dad is doing ok despite having lung cancer recently and Sarah, again, does all she can to look after him as well.

Throughout Millie's life she has always felt guilt. For the things she thought she could have changed and even for the things she can't.
It's now been 21 years since Millie brought her children to the Uk. Family and friends mean more to Mills than anyone could imagine. Distance makes you realise how important those people are. Death will become all of us, it's the moments you get along the way that matter.

Chapter 10

Dating nightmares

Millie thought about Neil and Ryan a lot, she was the type of person who wore her heart on her sleeve and became attached to people she cared about. She wanted to find love and wasn't about to give up her pursuit. Opening a dating app on her phone, Millie created a profile and eventually started talking to a few men in the area. Conversations dwindled quickly when one of them didn't feel they were a good match, but on the odd occasion Millie would end up with a date.

"Do you want to meet up for a drink?" She was asked by one man she had spoke to for a few weeks, Millie agreed and on that Saturday afternoon they agreed to meet at a local pub. Millie had rules when it came to dating. A way of keeping herself safe.

1. Meet in a public place, during the day.

2. Never let anyone pick you up from your home.

3. Do not get in anyone's car.

4. Always drive herself there so she had a way home.

5. Never have more than 1 alcoholic drink.

That date Millie drove herself to the pub and waited in the car until he sent a text to say he was there. They met in the car park and walked inside and ordered a drink. Millie only had a diet coke while her date ordered a beer. When he went to pay, he pulled out a bag of coins from his pocket. He began counting small change. Millie's eyes widen with embarrassment, he was literally counting 20 and 10ps. Embarrassed, she pulled out her bank card and paid for the drinks. In most cases, Millie was fine letting the man buy the first drink and Millie would always get the second round. She wasn't bothered paying, she was simply dumbfounded, like had he raided his sofa cushions prior to the date?
There wasn't going to be a second date that's for

sure. She stayed and chatted politely for an hour, then excused herself and went home.

Millie experienced being ghosted (when men just stop replying to texts and disappear for no reason), she was stood up a few times. Once Millie had suggested going to a comedy evening. Since she knew the venue Millie booked and paid for the tickets and they agreed that he would pay for drinks. She drove to the theatre and waited in the car park. When the show was about to start and her date had still not shown up, Millie's messaged him. "Are you fucking kidding me," Mills said to herself. He had blocked her number.

She didn't have the nerve to go in herself so Millie accepted it as a loss and drove home.

Some men on the app, were overflowing with confidence and were eager to send unsolicited dick pics.
The most horrible situations for her though were when they told Millie wasn't good enough, that hurt the most.

She was too fat.

She had children.

She didn't own her house.

She didn't have a career.

Hell, Millie was even told she should be more of a lady and wear dresses and high heels all the time. Heels were a definite no go! Millie's knee was even more messed up now, over the years Mills had torn her meniscus twice and had surgery on each occasion. She was still getting around ok, but she definitely could not wear high heels.

Mills had put on weight, a combination of having children, stress and not being able to exercise much. That was her biggest self-confidence issue.

"My ex was only a size 8."

"You're a bit bigger than I thought."

"You should exercise more."

Millie had heard it all. Gone were the days of her slim body, her high-spirited self, her blonde hair blowing in the wind as she stood by her favourite lake, laughing.

"Everyone has someone, you just have to find them." Advice from Paula.

"They aren't worthy of you if they don't like you for you." Advice from Lily.

They were both right but there were days Millie just felt like she was meant to be alone.

After going through periods of dating, giving up, dating again and giving up again, Millie took some advice after speaking with Ryan.

"You deserve someone better," Ryan had told her. Millie did love Ryan but it wasn't to be and maybe he was right. Maybe she needed to find someone who did want her.

She soon found herself speaking with a man named George. George was Millie's perfect type, he was black, tall, and built like a brick shit house, as her mom would say. Basically, that meant he was shaped like a rugby player. On their first date, they met, at Millie's local pub. George even brought flowers, which Millie had only received one time before in her life. They sat outside and had a drink speaking for hours. George was funny, kind and reminded her of a big bear with marshmallow insides.

George and Millie met up often, they went to the movies, out for dinner, George even took her to his caravan where he was living. He had most of his belongings in a storage garage and took Millie there to show her his collection of car models. He and his wife had been separated for nearly two years.

One date George and Millie shared, he took her for a drive, they ended up outside a wooded area. It was getting dark and Millie felt a little uncomfortable.

"What are we doing here?" She questioned him

"Trust me," George replied, his smile always won her over.

Nervous and a bit unsure about walking into the dark woods with a man she had only know a few months, was very stupid. Millie would ring Erica's neck if she ever did such a thing. For some reason though, Millie took his hand and walked into the woods. He led her through a short trail into an open area.

"Look up," George said, putting his arm around Millie. She did as he said and leaned back into him while looking up to the sky. The trees folded across each other leaving a small hole in the centre where Mills could see the sky. It was like a tunnel to the stars. It ended up be a beautiful experience, a stupid thing to do, but a beautiful experience in the end.

After four months of seeing George, Millie missed her period. She took a pregnancy test and was gobsmacked to see the two pink lines. She was 42 years old now and definitely wasn't expecting to be a mother again. Erica was approaching her 21st birthday, Jason was 19 and Riley would be 16 soon. She had her freedom now, with the kids being older. Was she ready to start all over again? Millie never believed abortion was an option for her. Although it was a big surprise, it was a good one. Millie definitely loved being a mom and she wasn't ready to hang up motherhood quite yet.

Mills told the children she needed to speak to them, She told them about her having a baby but she wasn't sure what they would say. They were shocked but Millie was convinced they would come around more when the baby was here.

Millie told George about her positive test over a coffee at Starbucks, she was 6 weeks along now and needed to book her first doctor's appointment. "That's exciting," he responded. She was happy he seemed pleased.

The next day before Millie even got out of bed she had an unexpected Facebook message. An older lady, with blonde hair had contacted her. It turned out to be George's wife! Apparently, George was still completely married, his caravan turned out to be his stud shack, where he went when he was wooing the ladies away from his wife's eyes. Millie was humiliated. Her doctors appointment came and went and George just backed out of the picture completely. He was happy to plant his seed and then walk away.

As Millie was an older mom, she had a few complications that of course she faced alone. She became gestationally diabetic, and her blood pressure was higher than normal, a c section was planned as doctors thought it would be safer due to Millie's age.

They wanted to know the sex of the baby, as Erica was planning a gender reveal party. Millie reached out to George and convinced him to at least find out if the baby was a boy or girl. George and Erica watched the screen as the ultrasound revealed the baby's sex. Millie closed her eyes as she was going to be surprised in a few weeks at the party.

The gender party was amazing, so many friends showed up and enjoyed food, drink and games. As it was October the gender reveal was a painted pumpkin. Millie had to lift the top off of a big white pumpkin and inside would be a baby pumpkin, painted either pink or blue.

The moment came and everyone stopped what they were doing to watch. The lid came off the large pumpkin, Millie reached inside and pulled out a PINK pumpkin baby.

"It's a girl!" Erica yelled out just as her mom set the baby pumpkin down on the table.

Jason and Rylie both wanted their mom to have a boy, but Erica was happy and so was Millie.

Millie still a month to go in her pregnancy but the baby had other ideas and labour started 4 weeks before her due date. Erica took her mom to the hospital and after a gruelling 3 hour wait, she was finally admitted. Kara was born only 6 lbs but chubby and beautiful . She was perfectly healthy besides being 1 day away from being premature.

Millie stared at Kara and knew she was the best thing that ever could have happened to her, she was blessed and so thankful Kara had come into her life.

Over the past few years, while dating, Millie had become promiscuous. She was, at times, so desperate to find love she had been doing things she wasn't proud of. Even in her 30s-40s Millie didn't realise sex didn't equal love.

Looking at the incredibly beautiful child now in her arms she knew Kara was giving her an opportunity to evaluate exactly what she deserved in life. She didn't have to be that scared child anymore, or the teenager who had been taken advantage of and she definitely didn't need to be the adult who still believed sex would give her love. She just looked at her daughter and promised to love her forever. She also promised to teach her to be caring, to be strong and to value her own worth.

Her own worth! Millie repeated those words in her head, realising she needed to discover that in herself as well.

Chapter 11

Learning to love herself

Millie had let go of believing she was worthy, she had been mistreated, abused and told she wasn't good enough for far too long.

"I'm raising four beautiful humans, all by myself, I'm kind, I'm caring, I'm generous, I'm a good friend. If someone can't see the beauty in me then fuck them!" Millie reminded herself on a daily basis that regardless of what other people thought, she was worth it!

If only it was that easy to change your entire outlook on life.

Mills received a call from Paula one day, that Paula's mom had taken ill, she was diagnosed with breast cancer.

Without a second thought Millie knew she wanted to do something, she couldn't just get on a plane and be with them, but she could help in another way. Millie and Erica worked together to raise money to help Paula's family with the expenses of travelling to the hospital to undergo chemo treatments, or anything else they may need. After raising a few hundred dollars the time was here? They turned on Facebook live, Erica got the hair trimmer and Millie's head was shaved, in front of family and friends. This was no small feat as Millie's hair hung halfway down her back.

Having a baby and shaving her head, Millie was making sure she wouldn't be dating for a good few years. At the same time she was proving to herself that she had a beautiful heart and she needed to see that more than anyone else did.

As Kara started to grow, Millie started to realise just how good of a mother she was, not trying to toot her own horn or anything, but she was doing a damn good job of raising her children alone. Raising a newborn baby alone!

One night when Kara decided 3am was playtime, Millie gave up on sleeping, she lay her baby on the bed and let her play with her hands, make raspberries into the air and goo at the shadows on the ceiling. Millie made a coffee and started to write.

"My parents moved home , a lot. They fought, a lot. I was abused as a child. As a teenager I was raped. Physical, emotional and sexual abuse engulfed my first marriage. I had horrible thoughts of murder. I was lied to, cheated on and gave up everyone I knew and loved. I left my home for someone who didn't value me. I was someone's unintentional mistres and I allowed men to take advantage of me. I was called names, put down, treated like I wasn't good enough!"

FUCK THEM!

Millie wasn't perfect, she knew she had flaws, she was clingy, she found it hard to trust, she would put roadblocks in situations where there didn't need to be. Her wall was built high and because of that people found it hard to get close to her. But all she wanted was for someone to love her.

Today Millie is nearing her 50th birthday. She is still a single mother. She's opening her heart to dating again, but this time she is a lot more careful with the selection process. She still battles her own demons and finds the need to do this on her own. Millie still hasn't lived out her dream of a happy marriage and finding the man of her dreams but she has fulfilled one dream she had from the time she was a little girl.

Shes writing her story. In her own words and in her own way.

Chapter 12

Lifes lessons

Millie still thinks a lot about the nearly 50 years she's been on the planet. There is so much to learn and so many lessons we have all had to endure. Thinking back over her life, this is what she has learned.

1. There are bad people out there and they should be held accountable for their actions.

2. People can change, but to do that, their circumstances have to change.

3. Friendship needs to be nurtured and if treated right they can last a lifetime.

4. You should never break a promise, you word is your bond.

5. You have a responsibility to your child, everyday, for the rest of your life. That goes for for moms and dads

6. Know and value your own self worth.

7. You deserve to be happy, to feel sexy and to see your own beauty inside and out. No one should take that from you.

8. Have a least one passion in life.

9. Do something nice for someone else everyday.

10. It takes a whole village to raise a child.

11. Never be afraid to fall in love. Start fresh with every new relationship,

12. Not everyone will want you, not everyone will like you. That's ok.

13. Appreciate the beauty in the world and in everything around you.

14. Take time for self reflection.

15. Learn from your own mistakes.

16. Never be afraid to say no.

17. Always take the opportunity to dance in the rain.

18. Allow people to make mistakes, we are all human and no one is perfect.

19. Pain is always only temporary.

20. Be proud of the person you are and never apologise for that.

Helpful Information

If anything is this book affects you, please reach out to the helplines available in your area.

NSPCC (UK). 0808 800 5000

Child Protection (Canada) 1-877-341-3101

Sexual abuse (over 16, UK) 0808 500 2222

Kids Help Phone (Canada) 1-800-668-6868

Suicide Prevention (Samaritan UK) 116 123

About the author

My name is Leona Kathleen Prevett. It has been a dream of mine since I was very little to become a writer. This has been my biggest passion and at 49 years old, my first official novel. Some details in the book are based on personal experiences and some are not. Names have been changed where necessary. I grew up in a beautiful little town called Walkerton, in Ontario Canada. I moved to the Uk in August of 2003. I have four children who are my absolute world. Alyssa Chelsea Moore, Zachary Charles Scott Moore, Rachel Stacy Hughes and Peyton Aryla-Gray Prevett. Life has thrown me many challenges and I proud to say I came

If anything in this book affects you personally, please seek help. Too many children and adults alike do not speak up when faced with abuse of all types. You are deserving of peace!

Thank you.

Leona K Prevett

Myself, Millie (Leona)

Erica and Jason (Alyssa and Zachary) in their school uniforms for their first day of school in England.

143

Leona with Rylie (Rachel)

Millie and Erica (Leona and Alyssa)

Jason and Kara (Zachary and Peyton)

My four babies

My cover girl Mollie (Alyssa's best friend)

Millies mom with Erica and Jason

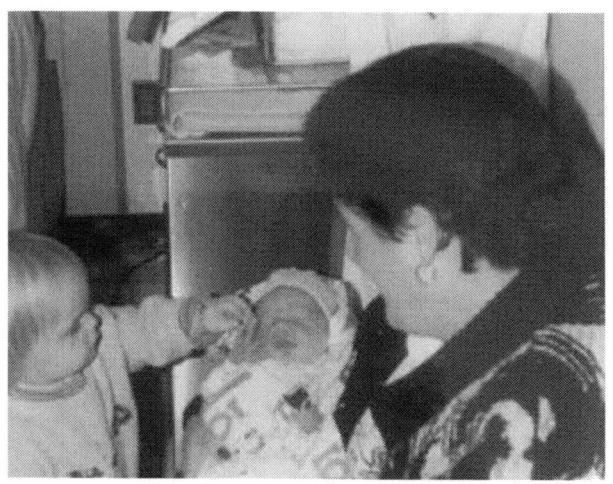

Erica and Rylie (Alyssa and Rachel)

Erica (Alyssa)

Kara (Peyton)

My mom, dad, sister, brother and me

My sister and her son (micheal)

149

Manufactured by Amazon.ca
Bolton, ON

39591692R00083